NATIVE AMERICA

A MAN CA

SITTING BULL

By

Carol Dean

ABOUT THE AUTHOR

 My name is Carol Dean and I'm married with two adult children, and three grandchildren and we all live in the North East.

I started to write children's stories to entertain my children when they were young on rainy weekends or school holidays. My son writing stories about ghosts or vampires, and my daughter drawing pretty pictures. Nothing to do with the story but very pretty.

And this is where my **Granny Ridley** and **Charlie Dryden** stories first appeared.

Charlie Dryden's crime/adventure stories have since developed into an exciting series of books for 9-15 year olds. My funny **Granny Ridley** series for 7-10 year olds now has a further nine books. Plus **PC Polly**, my commissioned work, has since made an amusing addition for 7-10 year olds to have a good giggle over.

Many other characters have appeared and entertained various age groups, (adults included) in the shape of dinosaurs, spiders, teddy bears, a panda, unicorns, with a friendly ghost there too. I am delighted to say that my books are popular in many countries around the world. Literally worldwide which is brilliant.

All of which you can find out more about on my website www.caroldeanbooks.com or follow me on Facebook.

Cover Image by Charles Marion Russell from Wikipedia

ISBN: 979-8-55089-754-6

ALSO BY CAROL DEAN

GRANNY RIDLEY SERIES

Granny Ridley Tries Exercise
Granny Ridley Knows the Way
Granny Ridley Goes on a Trip
Granny Ridley in the Snow
Granny Ridley and the Alien

Granny Ridley Helps Out
Granny Ridley Tries Knitting
Granny Ridley Has a Weekend Away
Granny Ridley and Wolfie
Granny Ridley Gets the Runs

CHARLIE DRYDEN SERIES

Charlie Dryden's Cricket Ball
Help Me Charlie Dryden
Charlie Dryden Finds a Bone
Charlie Dryden and the Charnwood Abbey Ghost
Charlie Dryden and the Guardian
Beware Charlie Dryden
Charlie Dryden and the Stolen Roman Standard

REAL FAIRY TALES

The Real Cinderella Story
The Three Bears and a Girl Called Goldie

DINOSAUR STORIES

Spotty the Dinosaur
Terry Comes Out of His Shell
Spike Gets a New Sister
Deano and the Baby Dinosaur

Deano Has Lost His Roar
Reggie Learns a Lesson
Herbie's Big Day

STORIES FROM DAYS GONE BY

Sophie the Suffragette

PC POLLY

PC Polly the Police Lady
Be Safe Be Seen PC Polly

PC Polly on Patrol
PC Polly and the Mini Police

GHOST STORIES

The Day the Ghost Got Scared

CHRISTMAS STORIES

Santa Steams Ahead
Santa and the Magic Dust
The Day Santa Met Santa

YOUNG READERS

Peter the Panda is Hungry
Webster Swings into Action

Teddy Has Lost His Growl

MAGICAL STORIES

Amelia Flurry and the Legend of the Unicorn

NATIVE AMERICAN SERIES

Comanche Life
A Man Called Sitting Bull
Geronimo and Cochise – Two Apache Legends

WAR STORIES

Ponsonby-Smallpiece - The Legend

You can find all Carol's books on her website www.caroldeanbooks.com.

CONTENTS

FOREWORD

After thoroughly enjoying writing my book *"Comanche Life"* which mentions the life of a hero of mine Chief Quanah Parker, the last Chief of the Comanche, I decided to continue with my interest in Native American famous Chiefs with my new book, *"A Man Called Sitting Bull"*.

Again a book featuring a remarkable man and his determination to make a better life for his tribe the Hunkpapa, Lakota Sioux. Thwarted bitterly by the white man, promised so much by the white man who failed to deliver on many occasions and in many ways, and then forced into a life of hardship and despair on the reservation.

Sounds familiar? It probably does but despite of all the depravation and the constant loss of their tribal lands, and the white man's expansion into those lands, Sitting Bull is still a legend.

A legend worthy of remembering and honouring, and I hope through this book, that is exactly what I have achieved.

Enjoy.

Carol Dean

A Brief Timeline of Recent South Dakota Native American History (1800-Present)

I have also picked just a couple of the dates from the list *(in bold Italics – please see end of timeline)* to show you what we in England were achieving on those particular timelines.

1800 - At this time, the Great Sioux Nation presides over the northern part of the Great Plains. This region includes North and South Dakota, northern Nebraska, eastern Wyoming and south-eastern Montana.

1803 - This was the time of the Louisiana Purchase and the start of the expansion into the western regions of North America leading to a dramatic decrease in the buffalo population, an animal central to the Lakota way of life.

1866-68 - Red Cloud heads a winning fight closing off the Bozeman Trail, a passage that lead to the gold mines in Montana. This trail also ran straight through the traditional hunting grounds of the Teton.

1868 - The Great Sioux Reservation is established which included most of South Dakota west of the Missouri River. The Fort Laramie Treaty of 1868 that authorised this pledged the government to keep whites out of this territory.

1874 - Gold is discovered in the Black Hills by General George A. Custer's expedition. A flood of prospectors engulfed the region invading Indian territories and ways of life.

1876 - June 25th, General Custer attacked an Indian settlement. Sitting Bull, Gall, Crazy Horse and many Cheyenne leaders defeated Custer and the 7th Calvary at the Battle of Little Bighorn. Custer lost all 200 men in the battle.

1889 - US Congress passes an act in March that split the Great Sioux Reservation into six smaller reservations. Some tribes began performing a religious ceremony meant to remove the whites and bring back the buffalo and their traditional way of life. This was called the Ghost Dance.

1890 - On Standing Rock Reservation, Chief Sitting Bull is murdered. After this, Big Foot and his Minneconjou band seek refuge in Pine Ridge under Red Cloud. Over 250 members of the Big Foot band are massacred by the 7th Calvary on December 29th at Wounded Knee. This clash has often been called the last major conflict between the US Army and the Great Sioux Nation. Mass grave at Wounded Knee.

1924 - The Citizenship Act of 1924 makes all Indians born within the territorial limits of the US full citizens.

1934 - The Indian Reorganization Act accepts tribal governments as sovereign.

1973 - Wounded Knee village is taken and occupied for 71 days by members of the American Indian Movement.

1990 - George S. Mickelson, South Dakota Governor and several representatives of the nine tribal governments in the state announce 1990 as a Year of Reconciliation. In 1991, a Century of Reconciliation is declared.

10th December 1868 - The world's first traffic lights are installed in Parliament Square in London.

29th March 1890 - Blackburn Rovers win their fourth FA Cup with a 6-1 victory over Sheffield Wednesday in the final at Kennington Oval, London.

THE START OF A LEGEND

Public Domain Image

The Start of a Legend

"I am a red man. If the Great Spirit had desired me to be a white man he would have made me so in the first place. He put in your heart certain wishes and plans, in my heart he put other and different desires. Each man is good in his sight. It is not necessary for Eagles to be Crows. We are poor… but we are free. No white man controls our footsteps. If we must die…we die defending our rights."

In 1831 the Lakota Sioux, the Hunkpapa tribe, were delivered of a new warrior. A male child for Jumping Bull (could also be named Returns Again or Sitting Bull), who was a fierce warrior, and the child's Mother was named Her Holy Door.

They named the child Jumping Badger when he was born, then affectionately his Father nick named him Huneski (Slow) because of his 'careful and unhurried nature'. It was later that his name changed to the more familiar one of Sitting Bull, which he earned.

Jumping Badger also had two sisters called Good Feather and Brown Shawl Woman or Twin Woman. A half-brother named Fool Dog from an earlier marriage lived with his mother's people the Arikaras.

Jumping Badger was born in the area now known as Dakota near the Yellowstone River, present day Montana. The Sioux called this land 'Many Caches' because of all the food storage pits they had dug there for safe keeping.

As a baby Jumping Badger spent many hours in a cradleboard, wrapped tightly for warmth and safety, spending his days with his mother while she worked. Until he was about ten months old that is, when he would be allowed out to start the crawling/walking phase. It was around this time that he earned the nickname of 'Slow' because of his 'careful and unhurried nature'.

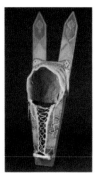

Birmingham Museum of Art
(https://commons.wikimedia.org/wiki/File:Cradleboard_of_the_Kiowa_or_Comanche_people.jpg)
Cradleboard of the Kiowa or Comanche people
https://creativecommons.org/licenses/by/3.0/legalcode

Public Domain Image

Sitting Bull's tipi and his family.

Life for Slow and many of the Plains Indians was virtually the same. A nomadic life, but I feel a very hard life. His home would have been a tipi made from many buffalo hides for warmth in the winter, and made so that it could be easily dismantled and transported when it was time to move on to follow the buffalo herds.

Tipis were literally buffalo hides stretched over a framework of poles. In really cold weather a fire would burn in the centre of the tipi, with the smoke drawn off through positioning of flaps at the top of the tipi.

In the summer cooking and sleeping would more than likely be outside with the tipi flaps open to allow a fresh breeze to cool the inside.

Her Holy Door, and her daughters, would have had many tasks to complete during the course of the day. Not just caring for Jumping Badger, but also working to help clothe and feed her husband and children and also to care for their elderly relatives too.

Preparing buffalo meat after a kill took a lot of time as nothing was left to go to waste. Even the bones were used to make knives and arrow heads with the sinews used as sewing thread. Nothing was wasted as you can see from the image.

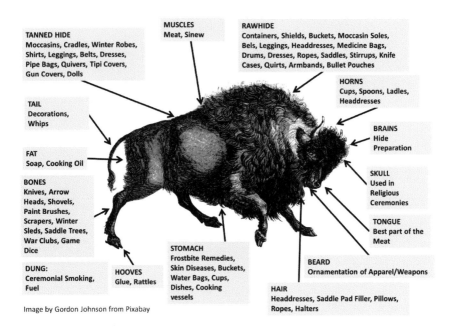

TANNED HIDE
Moccasins, Cradles, Winter Robes,
Shirts, Leggings, Belts, Dresses,
Pipe Bags, Quivers, Tipi Covers,
Gun Covers, Dolls

MUSCLES
Meat, Sinew

RAWHIDE
Containers, Shields, Buckets, Moccasin Soles,
Bels, Leggings, Headdresses, Medicine Bags,
Drums, Dresses, Ropes, Saddles, Stirrups, Knife
Cases, Quirts, Armbands, Bullet Pouches

HORNS
Cups, Spoons, Ladles,
Headdresses

TAIL
Decorations,
Whips

BRAINS
Hide
Preparation

FAT
Soap, Cooking Oil

SKULL
Used in
Religious
Ceremonies

BONES
Knives, Arrow
Heads, Shovels,
Paint Brushes,
Scrapers, Winter
Sleds, Saddle Trees,
War Clubs, Game
Dice

TONGUE
Best part of the
Meat

DUNG:
Ceremonial Smoking,
Fuel

HOOVES
Glue, Rattles

STOMACH
Frostbite Remedies,
Skin Diseases, Buckets,
Water Bags, Cups,
Dishes, Cooking
vessels

BEARD
Ornamentation of Apparel/Weapons

HAIR
Headdresses, Saddle Pad Filler, Pillows,
Ropes, Halters

Image by Gordon Johnson from Pixabay

Buffalo meat was their staple diet, but they did mix it with berries which made a high energy food for the children or the hunters, and it was called pemmican. Plus a good supply was always there for food shortages.

But they would also hunt for elk, bear, antelope, deer, armadillos, skunks, rats, lizards, frogs and grasshoppers too, as well as nuts and berries and sometimes honey for flavouring.

But it would be a long time before Slow would be part of the hunt. He had the privilege of enjoying his life as a Hunkpapa boy with no real tasks to perform. Not yet anyway.

Sioux children were called "Wakanisha" which meant sacred and were the centre of attention. Slow was no different growing up as any child would within the tribe, learning from his Uncle Four Horns, how the horses came to the Plains way back in his grandfather's time, making life so much easier. Using dogs to pull travois when moving camp, was a hard job. But the horses made such a difference. Everything was a lot quicker by horseback and more could be carried.

Hunting buffalo was simplified as the speed of the horse and the expert Sioux rider could follow the buffalo at speed and shoot from the horse's back with tremendous accuracy.

Public Domain Image

Slow needed to learn the art of riding, and did so early on in his life, mastering it quickly. He loved horses and apparently owned quite a few too when he got older.

When he was older he had the skill to ride in battle without a saddle or a bridle, and be able to slip from one side of the horse to the other flattening himself against the horse to dodge arrows or bullets. Riding like this in battle made for a smaller target hanging onto the horse's mane with his hands and his legs around the trunk of the horse. This enabled him to shoot a pistol with greater accuracy and protect himself into the bargain.

His favourite horse was apparently a sorrel (sorrel is a reddish colour for a horse's coat) called Bloated Jaw or Lump on the Jaw. It was stolen from a white man (Wasichus) and it always got him there first in battles or hunting.

As with all young braves, it was necessary to train in the bow and arrow. Not just for hunting which was very important, but also to be a true Sioux you must help and protect the people. The best way for a Sioux to gain the respect of the people was to be both brave and wise.

Hunting may have started off with small animals to supply the tribe with extra meat, but more importantly hunting buffalo helped to provide for his tribe for many long winters. Slow always wanted to do his best, so that one day he could become a great warrior for his tribe.

Slow proved himself big style when at the tender age of ten he managed to kill his first buffalo, a yearling calf. His mother skinned the calf and with her daughter's help, made the hide into a robe for Slow. His vision of manhood for himself was like that of many others boys of his age, waiting for the day when he could meet an enemy and beat him in combat.

He learnt, from listening to the older warriors in the tribe, their stories of battle. Life was good. Life was exciting.

Within the Sioux Nation were several tribes that speak different languages, The Lakota, Dakota and Nakota. The name "Sioux" is short for Nadowessioux, meaning "little snakes", which was a spiteful nickname given to them by the Ojibwe, their longtime foe. The fur traders abbreviated this name to Sioux which is now commonly used. But the Sioux prefer to call themselves Lakota or Dakota meaning 'friends, allies or to be friendly'. With no disrespect intended I am using the name Sioux throughout this book as they themselves are now known as The Great Sioux Nation.

The Lakota were also called the Teton Sioux and were the most powerful and the largest Nation. They lived in the both North and South Dakota.

The Dakota, or Santee Sioux, lived in Minnesota and Nebraska, whilst the Nakota stayed around South Dakota, North Dakota and Montana.

As a tribe the Lakota (which is sometimes spelt 'Lakhota') had seven strands to it, and they were known as warriors and buffalo hunters. The name Tetons indicated their location and language, but they were sometimes known as that too. The seven tribes making up the Lakota were:
 ➢ Ogalala ("they scatter their own," or "dust scatterers")
 ➢ Sicangu or Brule ("Burnt Thighs")
 ➢ Hunkpapa ("end of the circle"), **Sitting Bull's tribe**
 ➢ Miniconjou ("planters beside the stream"),
 ➢ Sihasapa or Blackfoot (confused with the separate Blackfoot tribe)
 ➢ Itazipacola (or Sans Arcs: "without bows")
 ➢ Oohenupa ("Two Boilings" or "Two Kettle")

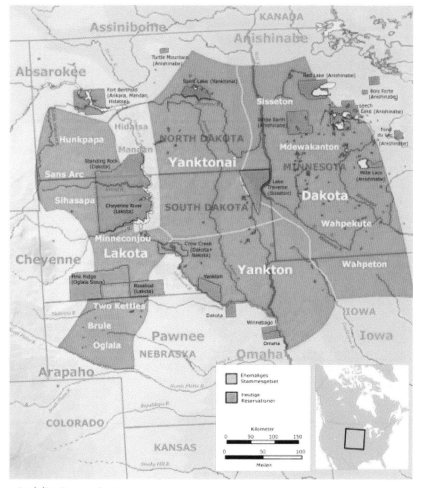

Public Domain Image

The Dakota Sioux were also called the Santee Sioux and moved to Minnesota. They had four bands;
➢ Mdewakantonwon
➢ Wahpeton
➢ Wahpekute
➢ Sisseton

The Nakota, also known as the Yankton Sioux left the Dakota tribe and moved to the prairies in South Dakota. They had three bands;
➢ Yankton
➢ Upper Yanktonai
➢ Lower Yanktonai

William Morris (https://commons.wikimedia.org/wiki/File:Louisiana_Purchase.jpg)
https://creativecommons.org/licenses/by-sa/4.0/legalcode

Since their first meeting with the Lewis and Clark Expedition in 1803, (an expedition to map the area known as the Louisiana Purchase for white settlers to inhabit), the Sioux have played a prominent part in the history of the northern plains and the state of South Dakota. Today, the descendants of the earlier Sioux nations can still be found on many of the reservations in South Dakota.

As a nation they believed in following the four cardinal virtues. Bravery, Fortitude, Generosity, and Wisdom.

Bravery was the biggest virtue for a warrior and war honours came when a warrior fearlessly risked his life and won the admiration of the tribe. He then would receive the greatest honours for his deeds.

First coup, hitting an enemy with the coup stick, was more daring than killing from a distance. So a warrior with many coup, would boast about it and if this was confirmed by the others there, then the warrior would receive an eagle feather to wear with pride. Slow was encouraged to show bravery from a very early age.

Fortitude came about by being able to endure extreme pain and discomfort such as torture or the sun dance, the steam of the sweat lodge that was past boiling point, injury inflicted by an enemy or broken bones during a buffalo hunt. Whatever form the discomfort came, they had to bear it without showing any signs of distress. Sounds impossible to me.

As an example, Sitting Bull's limp came from combat with a Crow warrior where he was challenged to face to face battle. Both had muskets, and Sitting Bull was able to get a quick shot off first, hitting the Crow in the stomach and killing him.

The Crow's shot (he had managed to fire before he died) ripped through Sitting Bull's shield turning downwards and hitting him in the foot ripping a furrow from toe to heel. Sitting Bull limped over to the Crow, scalped him, got on his horse, rode away and did not show any signs of discomfort or distress (fortitude). The wound did not heal properly and he always walked with a limp after that.

Fortitude was also showing dignity and reserve especially in emotional circumstance such as at a council meeting. No signs of humour or excitement had to be shown as there was a time and a place for such things. Just not then and there.

Generosity was a big one too for the Sioux as people mattered more than property. If you had a lot of possessions this would be viewed by others as disgraceful. Respect and admiration came from giving away your property to those who were orphaned or crippled or old. If you have more than enough, give it to them. This happened with horses and food too.

Wisdom is the final virtue and this as always comes with age and experience. Possessing wisdom meant that a man had superior judgement regarding war, the hunt, tribal policy and relationships. So maturity was something that the Sioux respected and they listened to their elders.

The Sioux are a deeply spiritual people, who believe in one god, Wakan Tanka the Great Mystery, or sometimes the Great Spirit. Religious visions were quite common and very important and the people communed with the spirit world through their music and dance. They did practise rituals of self-sacrifice, by slashing themselves or inflicting wounds on their body, to show or prove that they were brave warriors. Slashing their arms, legs or chest was also practised by mourners during burial ceremonies.

Slow's father had the ability to communicate with the spirit world through animals or dreams and could hear and understand the animals' words. Some warriors were not only exceptional fighters, but also had this ability too. Slow was gifted this way too.

He very quickly established himself as a skilled hunter and an exceptionally brave warrior. Because of his skills in the spirit world, he earned the title and role as the *wichasha wakan*, or holy man (dreamers). He could interpret visions from those during a vision quest (a boy's rite of passage to manhood) and dreams from the spirit world.

Once a boy had performed his vision quest and had perhaps found his guiding power in the form of an animal such as the bear (strength) after fasting for four days until the vision came, he then would return to the tribe and speak with the holy man who would help to harness that special power in order to have strength and protection from then on.

At the age of fourteen, Slow was allowed to be part of a raiding party to a camp of the Crow tribe, along with his Father and his uncle Four Horns. They wanted horses. His father presented Slow with a coup stick (a long pole with which to strike your enemy and gain the respect of the tribe).

Slow showed great courage by riding forward and counting coup, (touching an enemy with your hand, bow or coup stick, or stealing their weapons and riding away safely) on a surprised Crow enemy warrior. This act was witnessed by the other Hunkpapa warriors

Public Domain Image

On their victorious return his father gave a feast and Slow was given a new name. The name, Tȟatȟáŋka Íyotake, which in the Lakota language means "Buffalo Bull Who Sits Down", and would later be abbreviated to "Sitting Bull". Sitting Bull would count coup more than sixty times gaining much respect from the Hunkapa tribe.

Sitting Bull's father also changed his name to Jumping Bull, and the entire band witnessed Sitting Bull being presented with his first eagle feather to wear in his hair with pride, plus a warrior's horse and a buffalo shield.

Shields were said to give their users sacred power. Sitting Bull inherited his father's shield which had the design of one of his father's visions and had been carefully crafted and painted with an image of this vision. It was coloured red, green, dark blue and brown with something bold and striking as the image. Could have been a bird, as with this image, or something more significant to his father.

Public Domain Image

The boy was now a man and a recognised Lakota Sioux warrior.

There are different explanations for his new name and all could be true. This is one from the book *'Living in Two Worlds'* by Charles Eastman:

> *"It is told that after a buffalo hunt the boys were enjoying a mimic hunt with the calves that had been left behind. A large calf turned viciously on Sitting Bull, whose pony had thrown him, but the alert youth got hold of both ears and struggled until the calf was pushed back into a buffalo wallow in a sitting posture. The boys shouted: 'He has subdued the buffalo! He made it sit down!' And from this incident was derived his familiar name of Sitting Bull."*

Sitting Bull also became well known because he took a captive from the Assiniboine tribe, saved the boy's life, and adopted him as his brother naming him Hohay. Hohay became completely devoted to Sitting Bull and over the years, when Sitting Bull had ceased going to war, would act as his representative in battle. It is said that for every brave deed Hohay performed he would announce aloud *"I, Sitting Bull's boy, do this in his name."* What utter devotion.

Sitting Bull was married quite a few times as was the practise amongst the Plains Indians. His first wife Light Hair, died in 1853 giving birth to a son, and Sitting Bull was twenty two at the time. Sadly he lost a four year old son in 1857, but adopted two children perhaps to take his son's place, again something that would happen in those days. Perhaps the children were white captives as they were often taken to replace a child that had died in the tribe. Or perhaps he adopted children from the tribe who had lost their parents. Who can say as it's all speculation on my part but he took them on and cared for them. That's the part I really like.

He married again at the age of 40 after throwing Snow on Her out of the tipi due to the constant bickering between her and Red Woman. Red Woman died in 1871 leaving a son and two daughters. In 1872 he chose Four Robes who had a widowed sister Seen by the Nation who had two sons. He married her too. They produced five more children.

Both sisters got on well with each other and married bliss returned.

Von Bern https://commons.wikimedia.org/wiki/
File:Sitting_Bull_and_Family_while_at_Fort_Randall_summer_or_fall_1881.jpg
https://creativecommons.org/licenses/by-sa/4.0/legalcode
Her Holy Door (his Mother) and one of his daughters, Many Horses

His wives were named:

➢ Four Robes

- ➢ Scarlet Woman
- ➢ Snow on Her
- ➢ Seen by Her Nation
- ➢ Light Hair

Two of his children were a son, Crow Foot, and a daughter, Many Horses.

Public Domain Image

Sitting Bull's Family Tipi

But before all this domestic bliss happened, Sitting Bull, as a young man aged twenty five, became a leader of the *Strong Heart*, an elite warrior society and, later, a distinguished member of the Silent Eaters, a group concerned with tribal welfare.

The *Strong Heart* was the most admired of the groups and Sitting Bull became one of the two bonnet wearers, or sash bearers, which made them pretty high ranking members of this elite group.

The sash bearers carried a picket pin and rope and during a battle they were expected to position themselves with the pin and the rope to the ground and remain there during the fighting, or until released by a tribe warrior, or killed by the enemy. Very brave or just dangerous. Or both.

A headdress consisted of a skullcap with buffalo horns and a long trail of eagle feathers. As a distinguished member of the elite *Strong Heart*

Society, Sitting Bull wore a buffalo hat with four feathers at the back, a weasel skin and a feathered lance. Other members of this elite society were Gall and Crow King.

Public Domain Image

Gall

Public Domain Image

Crow King

A further society was called the *Silent Eaters* which was a secret group announcing meetings quietly through member to member. They would meet at midnight and feast on the best cuts of buffalo or sit and discuss tribal issues.

There was also the *White Horse Riders* which were a highly visible society and founded in 1875. Although its members were skilful warriors and excellent hunters, they still had to be generous and take care of any orphans in the tribe.

They had to obey direct orders of Chiefs and had brilliant battle skills. The society also organized tribal hunts when buffalo had been sighted.

Sitting Bull was the Chief of the *Silent Eaters* and they staged many a colourful parade dressed in their finery and always painted their war deeds on their white horses, e.g. a red hand for an enemy killed or a hoof print for every captured horse. The horse would be decorated with beads and paintings and much singing to honour older braves during the celebrations.

Public Domain Image

They might also have been part of a personal police force for Sitting Bull to protect him, therefore confirming his authority when be became Chief of the Sioux.

Public Domain Image

As a tribal leader, Sitting Bull helped extend the Sioux hunting grounds westward into the territory of the Shoshone, Crow, Assiniboine and other Indian tribes. Food was important and worth fighting for.

Public Domain Image

Sitting Bull was described as *"about 5 feet 10 inches tall, with a muscular build, alert crow-like eyes, a broad pockmarked face, a prominent hooked nose and a firm mouth. He wore his hair in two long braids hanging down over his shoulders. He was bowlegged and walked with a limp."* It was also said of him jokingly that his legs were bowed *"like the ribs of the ponies that he rode constantly from childhood."* As an untutored man he still had the skills to captivate his listeners when speaking. He was a diplomat and although he stopped going on the warpath in his later years, he was an excellent counsellor for his people. He was described as, *"bull-headed; quick to grasp a situation, and not readily induced to change his mind. He was not suspicious until he was forced to be so. All his meaner traits were inevitably developed by the events of his later career."*

Very detailed and difficult to confirm. It also depends on your own point of view which you can decide upon once you have read the rest of this book.

Sitting Bull continued to impress and became Chief of the Hunkpapas in the 1860s, at a time of a mass invasion of the white man with their constant advancement on tribal lands. Every year saw their numbers increasing. Although his hope had been for peace with the white man, their disregard for his people, and the fact that they would not leave, meant that Sitting Bull and the tribe had to start to fight back big style. The year was 1863, and the Americans quickly learnt the name of Sitting Bull.

In June 1863, a campaign of total retaliation by the US Army for a rebellion (the Santee Rebellion in Minnesota) in which Sitting Bull and his people played no part at all, took place. The Sioux were starving and their annuities promised had not arrived, and the Indian agent on the reservation did not care either and reportedly said, "Let them eat grass."

A battle ensued as the Sioux, under Little Crow, attacked white settlers' homes and many, many white settlers lost their lives.

Major General John Pope was tasked with the duty of finding the Sioux culprits, which he did, all 303 of them, who were brought to trial and condemned.

Most of the sentences were commuted by President Lincoln but on December 26th 1862 thirty eight Sioux warriors were hung in a public execution as punishment for their part in the Santee Rebellion.

Public Domain Image
Major General John Pope

The following year Sitting Bull battled with US troops at the Battle of Killdeer Mountain. This was purely to punish all Sioux regardless of their involvement in previous battles (Dakota War 1862). And punish they did pushing the Sioux ever further away from their lands to make room for the white settlers.

At Killdeer Mountain the Sioux had made camp and their leader was Hunkpapa Lone Dog. But despite their battle skills, their bows and arrows were no match for the long range rifles and cannons of the military 'Long Knives'.

The Long Knives didn't fight like the Sioux, Sitting Bull realised this quite quickly, as they did not try to demonstrate bravery. The Long Knives fought in organised lines and groups all obeying what their leaders told them without question.

The Sioux, on the other hand, attacked from different areas making their attacks a surprise and brutal too, but their casualties were high. His uncle Four Horns was shot in the back and Sitting Bull administered first aid to help. The bullet was never removed but Four Horns said it did not bother him again when it had *'fallen into his stomach'*. Ouch! But fortitude again.

Flickr: Commercial Use Allowed

Although now beaten and their camp gone, they quickly re-established themselves in another location and many other tribes joined their cause against the military.

The hostilities continued for many years with attacks on the US Army due to their constant invasion of the Sioux hunting grounds.

In 1868 Sitting Bull refused to sign the Treaty of Laramie, one of three treaties, which would have sent them to live on a reservation where we now find present day South Dakota

Over the next few years Sitting Bull continued leading his warriors into raids against railroad workers and settlers along the Yellowstone River. Despite still trading with the white man occasionally, the white man had to stop travelling on their lands. If they didn't stop then they would have to be driven out.

Although already acknowledged as a leader of his people, as he had been their tribal Chief for eight years now, in 1869, famous for his bravery already and respected for his wisdom too, Sitting Bull became the Supreme Chief of the Lakota Sioux Nation. He chose Crazy Horse, the leader of the Oglala Sioux, as his Vice Chief.

Sitting Bull's skill as a leader united the Sioux tribes of the Great Plains and they fought as one against the white man trying to take their tribal lands.

A treaty was again formulated to try and ease the tensions between the white man and the Sioux in the form of the Fort Laramie Treaty in 1868.

The US granted the Sioux the right to use and have their sacred lands in the Black Hills of Dakota. Until gold was found in 1874 then the US Government decided the Sioux had to be removed and removed by force.

And the white settlers kept on coming. In 1870, there were 5,000 of them, with a further 15,000 soldiers at forts on the Sioux land. By 1880, 117,000 white men lived on the land designated as the Great Sioux Reservation.

The white man settled in, ploughed fields for wheat, and destroyed the buffalo migration paths. By 1885, the number of white settlers had doubled to 234,000. The Sioux were being squeezed out of their land and it just made them, understandably, want to fight all that harder to preserve what they had.

And the battles did continue with the now famous 1876 Battle of Little Bighorn. Sitting Bull and Crazy Horse led the united tribes to victory against General George Armstrong Custer.

As a Chief and a holy man, Sitting Bull remained solid in his defiance towards the US military and how they reneged on promises when it came to peace treaties.

"I have killed, robbed, and injured too many white men to believe in a good peace." Such were the very strong and truthful words of Hunkpapa Lakota Sitting Bull, born in 1831 near the shores of the Grand River located in the Dakota Territory. A holy man and tribal Chief but he knew there would never be peace.

TREATY

between the respective parties hereto, so far as such
treaties and agreements obligate the United States
to furnish and provide money, clothing or other
articles of property to such Indians and Bands
of Indians as become parties to this Treaty, but
no further.

In Testimony of all which we the said Commissioners and we the Chiefs and Head men of the
Brulé Band of the Sioux Nation have hereunto
set our hands and seals at Fort Laramie,
Lakota Territory this twenty-ninth day of
April in the year one thousand eight hundred
and sixty Eight.

Public Domain Image

Treaty

"No white person or persons shall be permitted to settle upon or occupy any portion of the territory, or without the consent of the Indians to pass through the same." Words of Peace Treaty 1868

In 1851 the Fort Laramie Treaty was set out to establish peace between the US Government and the tribes. Mainly because the US Government wanted to build roads and military posts on the Sioux land, and they promised to protect them from the white settlers.

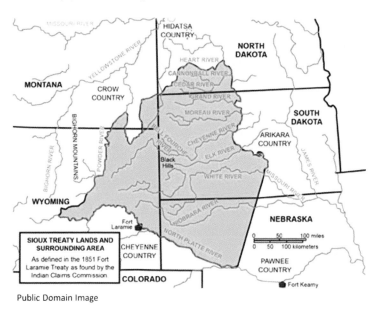

Public Domain Image

The US Government promised to provide annuities of $50,000 for 50 years. Then they re-thought this and made it 15 years.

But the treaty caused many a problem for the US Government as the officials just assumed that the Sioux understood what was going to happen, and as they had 'touched the pen', they therefore must understand. How naive is that?

Older leaders of the Sioux did seek peace with the white man, but the younger warriors like Sitting Bull, who was twenty two at the time, still wanted the honour of battle and stealing horses from their enemies, the Crow. They wanted status from the tribe, not peace and harmony.

So the hostilities continued and the enemies of the Sioux and Cheyenne (the Crow and the white man) were attacked many times.

Public Domain Image
Conquering Bear

One particular incident occurred when a very keen young Lieutenant, John L. Grattan, marched his troops into a Brulee village and demanded the surrender of a Miniconjou visitor in Conquering Bears camp.

The visitor had apparently killed an oxen that had strayed from a wagon train. This was never going to happen and he ordered his men to open fire on the camp. Conquering Bear was killed, as were all the soldiers. It was called the Grattan Massacre and paved the way for many more Sioux battles with the US military and the white man.

Retaliation came swift from the US army with many troops arriving around the area of Fort Pierre and attacks on Sioux camps killing women and children regardless. General William S. Harney was behind these attacks and the Sioux called him Mad Bear, as he just went mad when it came to any Sioux camp.

Public Domain Image
General William S. Harney

At the age of 26, Sitting Bull witnessed a peace treaty that General Harney had devised. Harney's treaty stated that any Indian that murdered any whites would be sent to the nearest military post for sentence; all stolen property had to be turned into a military post; all Indians had to keep away from white settlers and not molest them. If they did not comply then they would be arrested and sent to a military post for sentence. In return the US Government would resume their annuities, return prisoners, and protect them from the white settlers.

In order to make sure that all this happened, he was going to appoint a head chief, and if they didn't make sure that his orders were carried out then they would get the same treatment as Little Thunder which meant death. (Little Thunder took over from Conquering Bear, but was wounded and captured during the retaliation for Grattan Massacre.)

I think a huge lesson was learnt by Sitting Bull watching these negotiations happen, as it proved to him that the white man, in the shape of this soldier Harney, was so ignorant of Indian ways, yet he had such power to make sure that what he dictated actually happened. Dealings with the white man were a definite no-no for Sitting Bull now.

"From the 1860s through the 1870s the American frontier was filled with Indian wars and skirmishes. In 1865 a congressional committee began a study of the Indian uprisings and wars in the West, resulting in a Report on the Condition of the Indian Tribes, which was released in 1867. This study and report by the congressional committee led to an act to establish an Indian Peace Commission to end the wars and prevent future Indian conflicts. The United States government set out to establish a series of Indian treaties that would force the Indians to give up their lands and move further west onto reservations."

Although Sitting Bull had made a very determined effort to rid the lands of the white man with constant onslaughts, the white man just kept on coming.

He joined forces with Red Cloud, the leader of the Oglala Lakota, from 1866 -1868 whose battle plan was to attack the many US Army Forts in the area. Sitting Bull attacked many forts too and led numerous war parties against white settlers and other smaller forts in the area.

Public Domain Image
Red Cloud

The US Government seemed to have a change of heart and decided that they wanted peace, and agreed to close a few of its forts and the Bozeman Trail (short cut to the gold fields), to meet demands made by Red Cloud.

And Red Cloud was then persuaded by the US Government to stop the onslaught and sign the Fort Laramie treaty on July 2nd 1868 at Fort Rice near Bismarck, which he did.

"Along with Red Cloud a further 24 other tribal leaders signed with representatives of the US government including Lieutenant General William Tecumseh Sherman. The treaty created the Great Sioux Reservation and earmarked additional land for the Sioux in parts of South Dakota, Wyoming and Nebraska."

Public Domain Image

Sitting Bull did not agree with Red Cloud and refused to sign. And this gained Sitting Bull a tremendous amount of support and many followers plus he was made the Supreme Leader of the Lakota Sioux. The first person to hold such a title. The Arapaho and Cheyenne soon joined him too.

Public Domain Image

Tribal Leaders

So the treaty was signed in 1868 with the US Government. This time the US Government guaranteed the Sioux a reservation in what is now south-western South Dakota.

After the treaty was signed Sitting Bull, Red Cloud and Spotted Tail were invited along to Washington and had dinner with President Grant and other high fliers. They must have made a curious set of dinner guests.

The meeting of minds, I think, was to seal the terms of the treaty whereby the US Government had promised to keep away from the Black Hills as it was the Sioux's hunting ground and sacred to them. The white man's life was so different to the Sioux and Sitting Bull could see that the gulf was huge between them but wanted to play his part in the treaty itself.

But when the gold was discovered and the white man had reneged on the treaty immediately, Sitting Bull naturally lost his faith in the white man and his lack of honour. This shows very dramatically in a speech he made to his council and I quote;

"Behold, my friends, the spring is come; the earth has gladly received the embraces of the sun, and we shall soon see the results of their love! Every seed is awakened, and all animal life. It is through this mysterious power that we too have our being, and we

therefore yield to our neighbours, even to our animal neighbours, the same right as ourselves to inhabit this vast land.

Yet hear me, friends! we have now to deal with another people, small and feeble when our forefathers first met with them, but now great and overbearing. Strangely enough, they have a mind to till the soil, and the love of possessions is a disease in them. These people have made many rules that the rich may break, but the poor may not! They have a religion in which the poor worship, but the rich will not! They even take tithes of the poor and weak to support the rich and those who rule.

They claim this mother of ours, the Earth, for their own use, and fence their neighbours away from her, and deface her with their buildings and their refuse. They compel her to produce out of season, and when sterile she is made to take medicine in order to produce again. All this is sacrilege.

This nation is like a spring freshet; it overruns its banks and destroys all who are in its path. We cannot dwell side by side. Only seven years ago we made a treaty by which we were assured that the buffalo country should be left to us forever. Now they threaten to take that from us also. My brothers, shall we submit? Or shall we say to them: 'First kill me, before you can take possession of my fatherland!"

He proved himself to be an excellent speaker and from then on channelled his energies into representing the tribe in tribal affairs. He was strong and determined in his mission and his personality held the tribe together with his good counsel.

But things were to change very rapidly when the gold was found in 'them there hills' in 1870. The sacred lands of the Black Hills were now a target for the white man. And the US Government wanted the gold. All of it. And the only way they could get at it was to order all the Sioux that did not live in the confines of the reservation, to move there. Immediately!

Sitting Bull believed that the reservations were like being in prison and he did not want to be *'shut up in a corral'*.

Public Domain Image

US Commissioners

So the treaty didn't last long. Nor did the fact that the land called the Black Hills was sacred to the Sioux. It was now sacred to the US because the US wanted the GOLD. End of story and it all seemed reasonable to the US Government.

News of the gold travelled fast and the white settlers descended on the land and claimed it as their own.

Reneging on yet another treaty the US Government turned the tables and made the peace talks into a demand that the Sioux left the area by 31st January 1876, and join the reservation or they would be classed as enemies and be dealt with accordingly. A journey of about 240 miles in deep winter for Sitting Bull and his tribe. An impossible 'ask'.

Sitting Bull refused and instead recruited a force of Native Americans including Arapaho, Cheyenne and the Sioux and fought against General George Crook and won in the Battle of the Rosebud on June 17th 1876. Then he moved his warriors to the valley known as the Little Big Horn.

RAILWAYS

Public Domain Image

Railways

In the late 1860s Sitting Bull's band of Hunkpapa were relentless attacking white settlers and forts in the area.

These lands had not seen a huge amount of white settlers arriving mainly because it wasn't the best of areas to try and farm or live. It had incredibly cold winters, 10-40 degrees below zero, and the summers could just toast you alive. It was vast and open land making it impossible to shelter from the constant strong winds and water was a bonus if you could find it.

But it was perfect for the Sioux. It gave them the opportunity to hunt for buffalo, which was their main source of food and clothing. They could move to new hunting grounds following the buffalo whenever they needed to. Life was good. For a time.

Even with the small amount of white settlers now living there, it upset the status quo. Buffalo were not able to roam as they had done and their numbers dwindled as they moved on to different pastures. Sitting Bull spoke of this and his summary is from the heart.

Public Domain Image

"White men like to dig in the ground for their food. My people prefer to hunt the buffalo. White men like to stay in one place. My people want to move their tepees here and there to different hunting grounds. The life of white men is slavery. They are prisoners in their towns or farms. The life my people want is freedom."

But they kept on coming. So much so that the railways were now making surveys of the Sioux homeland to send the rail lines straight through Hunkpapa lands. They were not greeted warmly as you can imagine.

In 1871 the railroad sent surveyors to the lands to establish plans for the forthcoming rail tracks. This led to many more attacks on the surveyors which initially put them off working in the area.

They tried again later and still met with the same resistance when Sitting Bull attacked the survey parties. So much so that the surveyors actually left, only to return in 1873 with a military escort to protect them. So Sitting Bull fought harder.

In one battle his young braves kept a constant barrage of arrows and musket fire aimed purposefully at the military protecting the surveyors. Showing immense bravery, Sitting Bull, to the amazement of his tribe, collected his pipe and tobacco and walked into the open valley within sight of the military. Wearing a shirt, leggings, and two feathers in his hair, carrying his rifle and bow and arrows he sat himself down and shouted to the others to join him.

Public Domain Image

Then he filled his pipe and was joined by White Bull, Gets the Best Of and two Cheyenne warriors. It must have been a terrifying experience as they sat there taking their turns with the pipe and hearing the soldiers bullets whistling through the air so close to them, and watching as the dirt in front of them sprang up where a bullet had hit.

Sitting Bull said nothing. He just sat there and smoked. When the smoking was over, he calmly cleaned the pipe bowl, put the pipe back in the pouch and walked back to some very impressed tribesmen. The others ran back. So quickly that Gets the Best Of forgot his bow and arrows. To show his own bravery, White Bull went back and retrieved them for him. Sitting Bull's act here was always remembered as 'the bravest deed possible'.

"But the Panic of 1873, a time when the banking firm of Jay Cooke and Company, a firm heavily invested in railroad construction, closed its doors on September 18, 1873, ('a major economic panic swept the nation. ... Jay Cooke's firm had been the government's chief financier of the Union military effort during the Civil War) forced the Northern Pacific Railway's backers (such as Jay Cooke) into bankruptcy. This halted construction of the railroad through Lakota, Dakota, and Nakota territory." From www.pbs.org

But not for long.

GOLD

Gold

Take me back to the black hills
The black hills of Dakota
To the beautiful Indian country
That I love
Calamity Jane 1953 sung by Doris Day

To the beautiful Indian country that I love and that the Sioux loved too. The Black Hills of Dakota. Sacred to the Sioux and now it was literally a gold mine. It's 1874 and it's going to get messy as the Sioux fought back to save their land.

In the 1868 treaty, signed at Fort Laramie, the US Government appeared to understand that this land was sacred, allocated it to the Sioux, and promised it would be 'off limits' to any white settlers, and that the Black Hills were now a part of the Great Sioux Reservation, just for the Sioux.

Then a man called General George A. Custer was tasked with leading a military expedition from Fort Abraham Lincoln near Bismarck to look for gold in the Black Hills, and to find a suitable site for another military fort there. The expedition consisted of miners who were eagerly looking for gold. And they found it. This was going to be the salvation needed to restore the US finances after the huge slump that followed the Panic of 1873.

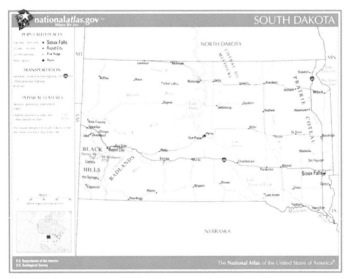

Public Domain Image

Public Domain Image

Soon the area was filled with thousands of miners hoping to strike it rich while destroying the area in their quest for gold. It was a dangerous life with the constant Sioux attacks on the miners there, and the miners demanded protection from the US Army. And they got it. The army was ordered to move the Sioux on any way that they could to secure the land. Tensions between the US Government and the Sioux were very high.

Public Domain Image

So the fighting continued. In an effort to make peace and gain the rights to the gold, the US Government offered to buy the Black Hills which the Sioux refused naturally. It was their land. And the Fort Laramie Treaty of 1868 was reneged.

Now any Sioux not on the reservation after 31st January 1876 were classed as an enemy to the US Government.

In the meantime many makeshift towns had sprung up for the gold miners and buffalo hunters in the area to spend their newly found fortunes.

Everything they could possibly want as far as supplies and anything else for that matter was concerned, at an exorbitant fee of course, could be bought there. With many other ways to lose your hard earned money, with the gamblers and cardsharps that frequented these places.

Deadwood was, and still is, one of those towns. Only now it's all for show to entertain the tourists. But in its heyday it was buzzing.

Public Domain Image

Public Domain Image

Deadwood

36

Public Domain Image

Meanwhile in his camp at Little Bighorn River, Sitting Bull as a holy man, "Wichasa Wakan," performed a Sun Dance ceremony, dancing for 36 hours and making 50 sacrificial cuts on each of his arms before going into a trance. He needed guidance from the Great Spirit to help his people.

This sun dance had a major impact on the tribe. Sitting Bull had made a vow to the Great Spirit to give his flesh for the protection of his people. After purifying himself in the sweat lodge, performing the pipe ceremony, he then sat down legs extended and arms resting on the ground, surrounded by buffalo robes.

Jumping Bull assisted this sun dance by starting at the bottom of Sitting Bull's left arm. He inserted an awl (a small pointed tool for piercing holes) beneath the skin and removed a piece of flesh about the size of a match head. He continued this until he had accumulated 50 pieces of flesh from the arm, then he started on the right arm doing the same process. Blood flowed everywhere. The whole process took about 30 minutes and it must have been hell.

All the time Sitting Bull chanted. Once it was over he danced and fasted whilst gazing into the sun seeking a vision. After many hours he suddenly stopped. Everyone present knew that something marvellous had happened and they gathered round him lowering him to the ground and waiting to hear his words.

37

Public Domain Image

During his trance he said he saw a vision of US soldiers falling like grasshoppers from the sky which, he explained, meant it was an omen that the army would be defeated. The tribe was exulted and ready to fight.

On June 17th 1876 despite the tribal council wanting to leave the soldiers under General George Crook, or Three Stars (because of the stars on either shoulder and one in his hat) alone, the young braves wanted to fight. And so did General Crook.

Although his men had had a very hard 35 mile walk and were extremely tired, Crook made no real decisions about protecting his troops from Indian attack. They were deep in the heart of Indian territory and probably feeling rather fidgety about the whole thing. And they should have been too.

Sitting Bull was unable to fight due to his arms still being very swollen from the sun dance, but he encouraged the others to continue the fight.

The Sioux and the Cheyenne attacked the troops from all angles and continued attacking relentlessly. It was a mishmash of tactics and plain bravery on both sides with neither side having a real battle plan.

But the bravery really belonged to the Sioux and the Cheyenne as they had taken on a much larger force than themselves in numbers, and although it wasn't a victory for the army, it wasn't a victory for the Sioux either.

But as Crook had used almost all of the ammunition brought along and knowing that he could not continue the battle without more ammo and reinforcements, he left with his troops, and the battle was claimed as a victory by the Sioux.

This victory encouraged even more to join the warriors and after only a few days the camp had doubled in size to 1,000 tipis, 7,000 people and 1,800 warriors. All were ready for battle.

As it turned out the next battle was at Little Big Horn.

CUSTER'S BATTLE OF LITTLE BIG HORN

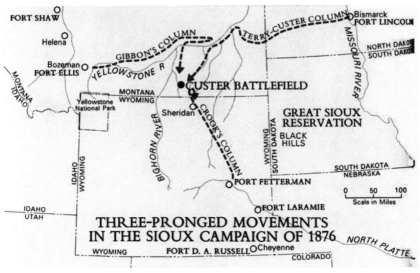

Public Domain Image

Custer's Battle of Little Big Horn

General George Armstrong Custer was tasked by the US Government to ensure those troublesome Sioux leaders Sitting Bull and Crazy Horse left the area and joined the reservation, leaving the Sioux lands open to everyone. Apart from the Sioux that is. And Custer was happy to oblige.

Public Domain Image

Custer's Crow Scouts

Sitting Bull, as far as the US Government was concerned, was stopping their plans for expansion into Native American lands. Something had to be done about him and his people. And quickly.

Sitting Bull's strategy was to fight back when it was needed rather than just attack for the sake of it.

A good idea but the US Government had a different approach and sent General Alfred H. Terry, Colonel John Gibbon and the seventh cavalry under Custer to meet and attack Sitting Bull's camp simultaneously.

Public Domain Image

General Alfred H. Terry

Public Domain Image

Custer's Indian Scouts

By this time Sitting Bull's vision had inspired seven thousand Lakota and Cheyenne to join his camp. Plus a victory at Rosebud River in Montana against General George Crook, where Sitting Bull's warriors had forced the army into a resounding retreat, and this had given them the boost that they needed for more battles with the army.

Public Domain Image
General Crook's HQ

Public Domain Image

After victory celebrations Sitting Bull moved the camp to Little Big Horn River. It was here that Sitting Bull performed the Sun Dance and the subsequent vision of *'soldiers falling into the camp like grasshoppers'* inspired his well established, and large numbers of warriors, to fight.

Public Domain Image

Then the 26th June 1876 arrived and Custer, who was rather keen to prove himself, was not prepared to wait until the General and the Colonel had arrived with their troops, and decided just to attack the camp.

But he hadn't realised how massive the camp was at Little Big Horn (or also known as Greasy Grass River to the Lakota), with all the tribes from the reservations now lodging there in support of Sitting Bull and Crazy Horse.

Public Domain Image

Public Domain Image
Crazy Horse

LIEUTENANT GRUMMOND SACRIFICING HIMSELF TO COVER THE RETREAT
Drawing by Charles Schreyvogel

Public Domain Image

Custer was undeterred and sent a battalion of men under Captain Frederick W. Benteen to scout south while Major Marcus A. Reno and

175 men advanced across the Little Bighorn River to face the enemy. Custer and his men, about 210 of them, turned right in formation to attack what looked to Custer like retreating 'Indians' and their dust clouds as they hurried away from the soldiers. Or so he thought.

Admittedly the Hunkpapa Sioux were trying to help the women and children escape to safety, and collect their horses, hence the huge dust cloud that all this activity was creating. The soldiers could be seen in the distance lining up to ready to fire on the camp following Custer's orders. They had to get the women and children to safety quickly.

With the might of the Hunkpapa Sioux, Cheyenne, Miniconjou, Sans Arc, Oglala, a few Blackfeet and Brulee working together the fight was on.

A great deal of fire was exchanged with the soldiers, from horse back and on foot too. And the soldiers kept on advancing. After a mounted charge by the Hunkpapas and the Oglalas, the soldiers managed to get into a covered area. The attack from the Hunkpapas and the Oglalas continued with a determined effort to get themselves behind the soldiers lines, pushing the soldiers into defensive bunches of small groups seeking cover.

This continued for some time and seemed to be organised chaos. Then the soldiers emerged from their covered positions and formed again. Or so it seemed but history has it that they started a hasty retreat. In the chaos the mounted tribesmen chased and charged the retreating soldiers knocking them from their horses and shooting them as they fled.

Military horses, scared by the confusion, bolted in every direction and some were stopped by women from the camp. As luck would have it the horses were still carrying their saddlebags which produced ammunition for the tribe to use along with the abandoned rifles lying next to their now dead or injured owners.

But it wasn't just the horses that ran, the soldiers had given up any attempt to keep a battle formation going and scattered. This made them very easy to pick off, and the warriors did just that.

Some soldiers managed to get to the river on their horses but the current in the river was too strong for them and many perished along with their horses. Others succeeded in heading up the hill to what they hoped would be safety. While others, less fortunate, were finished off by the women and young braves and their possessions claimed. Many were mutilated, as was the way for either the tribes or the white man. Both did terrible things to each other in the name of war.

One Bull – nephew and adopted son of Sitting Bull

But the fighting continued. The warriors had spotted another 'line of blue' and were now converging from all sides. Sitting Bull could see that this had left the women and children of the camp unprotected and was concerned that things could very quickly turn round on them. Sitting Bull and One Bull positioned themselves to see the battle and to protect the camp. Through the smoke and the dust Sitting Bull could see that the warriors were succeeding.

To the north the soldiers collected on a hilltop and could probably see that they were surrounded. Face to face combat, shooting at close range, fighting for your life, fending off tomahawks, trying to strike the enemy first. Trying to see through all the dust and smoke and hearing and fearing the whooping and yelling of the tribal battle cries as they got closer and closer. This was now the battle. The last stand.

47

Custer's 7th Cavalry had fought valiantly but were totally outnumbered. Custer had only succeeded in driving the tribes' bloodlust up with his surprise attack. The tribes' counter attack against the cavalry, surrounding them and killing all 209 of his troops, had not been how Custer had thought it would work out I am sure. Custer just didn't stand a chance. This was literally Custer's last stand.

Public Domain Image
General Custer

His horse would have been claimed as a great battle prize, as would the saddle and anything else that had been Custer's on the day he died. Many claimed to have killed him too. No-one really knows who did.

Four miles away, Major Reno and Captain Benteen had their own battle to fight as they encountered braves returning from the 'last stand' fight. At this stage the soldiers had only heard the noise of battle in the distance and were unaware that Custer had fallen. They defended where they were and fought for their lives too.

This battle continued with many more deaths and casualties. Sitting Bull, watching the proceedings from above, tried to call a halt to the battle by saying *"Let them go now, so some can go home and spread the news."*

The battle had fulfilled Sitting Bull's sun dance vision as soldiers had fallen into their camp and died. As the tribe celebrated with a victory dance, Sitting Bull was more reflective on the events and said, *"I feel sorry that too many were killed on each side, but when Indians must fight they must."*

The battle was considered as one of the greatest victories for the Native Americans against the US Army, but a stunning defeat for the US.

But who was to blame? The US Government needed someone to blame for this disaster. Was it Custer, Reno or Benteen? Or perhaps even President Ulysses S. Grant? It certainly was a bad judgement call as none of them thought for one minute that the 'Indians' would have such impressive battle tactics.

Public Domain Image
Custer's dead horses

It surprised them that the tribe numbers had been so high. Again they had assumed that the tribe would just be in a small band and easy to deal with. Their skill and intensity in battle also surprised the US army and their leaders, as they discovered that unlike the soldiers, who followed the orders of their commander to the letter, the tribe warriors followed their Chief because they wanted to. Yes they would fight for that Chief but he did not order them to fight. This showed exactly how little the US army knew and understood about the tribes. They won the Battle of Little Big horn because they worked together, and all held the same hatred and anger towards the soldiers. They fought to protect their families. And they won because the soldiers attacking strategy broke down, their morale collapsed, and discipline dissipated under the extreme pressure imposed by the various tribes that day.

The US Government tried to discredit Sitting Bull by saying he was not part of the battle at all. Sitting Bull's not playing a major fighting role in the battle would have been very acceptable by the tribes. Sitting Bull was forty five years of age, a Chief of many years, a counsellor and a very valuable holy man. He had proved his bravery many times in battle and no one questioned his bravery or honour this way. Chiefs themselves were only ever expected to fight when the women and children needed protecting. And he did just that.

He fought the soldiers under Reno to protect the camp, and although they retreated, instead of leaving himself, he continued to fire on the remaining soldiers alongside his younger braves.

He made his presence felt by staying in the thick of things while the battle with the soldiers led by Reno continued, shouting encouragement to his braves. He was, and still is, a hero. He had the white and red feathers presented to him for his bravery. The first of the cardinal virtues of the Sioux.

Public Domain Image
Cheyenne - Wooden Leg

Cheyenne Wooden Leg had this to say about Sitting Bull. *"I am not ashamed that I was a follower of Sitting Bull. I have no ears for hearing anybody say that he was not a brave man. He had a big brain and a good one, a strong heart and a generous one. In the old times I never heard of any Indian having spoken otherwise of him. If any of them changed their talk in later days, the change must have been brought about by lies of agents and soldier chiefs who schemed to make themselves appear as good men by making him appear as a bad man."*

Regardless of all this the American public were still outraged over this huge defeat.

Public Domain Image
Spotted Tail

Because of the outrage, the victory for Sitting Bull was short-lived as the US Government sent in more and more troops into South Dakota over the next year to pursue the Sioux and to avenge the death of Custer and his men. Sitting Bull was faced with being constantly pursued. General Sheridan organised 'total war' against them sending General Terry into

Standing Rock and the Cheyenne agencies to remove any firearms from the hunting parties. Similarly, General Crook dealt with Red Cloud and his band by removing their firearms and their horses, and replaced Red Cloud as leader with Spotted Tail instead. The US Government were determined to have total control.

Many of the Chiefs involved were forced into surrender and herded onto reservations. Sitting Bull, although still defiant, had to make the decision of death or survival.

Sitting Bull and his followers, the Hunkpapas, Miniconjous and Sans Arc needed buffalo meat but the US Government had decided that it was necessary to keep the Sioux moving away from the area or surrender.

In order to start this ball rolling it had been decided that a series of forts would be erected right along the main area of the buffalo trail. This naturally caused further unrest particularly on wagon trains, carrying freight, travelling the area. The constant attacks stopped the wagon trains for a while until 86 wagons protected by 200 heavily armed soldiers arrived. The Sioux attacked but were forced back because of the huge capacity of the soldiers long range rifles. The attack did not stop the wagon train.

A council had to be arranged to agree the next move and Sitting Bull took the initiative of writing a message, translated by Big Leggings, to leave in the middle of the road in the path of the wagon train tied to a stick.

The message read, ***"I want to know what you are doing travelling on this road. You scare all the buffalo away. I want to hunt on the place. I want to you to turn back from here. If you don't, I will fight again. I want you to leave what you have got here, and turn back from here. I am your friend. Sitting Bull. I mean all the rations you have got and some powder. Wish you would write as soon as you can."***

Big Leggings did the best he could to convey exactly how Sitting Bull was feeling I'm sure. But the council felt it would be better if he could actually speak to the US officers guarding the wagon train in a parley. It was arranged. But it didn't go well. Other Chiefs spoke and demands were made for ammunition and supplies. Lieutenant Colonel Elwell S. Otis was unhappy to assist but relented and gave them some food. Then he continued the journey with the wagon train. Unabashed.

Colonel Miles, in the meantime, was concerned that the wagon train was delayed and suspected an attack had happened and sped to the rescue. Miles encountered Sitting Bull who arranged another parlay with Miles this time.

Public Domain Image
Colonel Nelson A. Miles

Miles did not have an interpreter so the proceedings were very difficult and somewhat heated. Big Leggings came to assist as he could speak English fairly well. But Miles had one thing in his mind. The unconditional surrender of Sitting Bull and his tribes, leaving everything behind and joining the reservation. Sitting Bull wanted the soldiers to leave them alone. It was not going well.

The parley continued the next day but the conditions remained the same. Sitting Bull was angry with Bear Coat as they called him, and left with the others. Then the soldiers and the Sioux, prepared for battle.

The tribes split and some headed with Sitting Bull towards Missouri. Miles gave chase and caught up with the rest of Sitting Bull's bands. They surrendered to Miles and agreed to join the Cheyenne River Agency.

Sitting Bull's encounter with Miles was only the start. Miles was a man on a mission and Sitting Bull was at the heart of that mission.

Sitting Bull decided on survival for his remaining tribal people, His retreat led him to Canada in May 1877 which was out of reach for the US army. Sitting Bull and his people had safety there.

But the US were relentless in their pursuit of the ownership of the Black Hills and continued to battle against the Sioux. Eventually in 1877 the land was confiscated but even now the ownership of the Black Hills remains a very controversial legal dispute between the US Government and the Sioux.

CANADA

Public Domain Image

Canada

Sitting Bull's refusal to surrender led him and the rest of his people to the North Western Territory, Canada in May 1877. To the White Mother's country as he called it.

US military battles with the Sioux and the Cheyenne had not gone on without attracting the attention of Commander James Morrow Walsh, (called White Forehead by Canadian Natives), of the North West Mounted Police, who felt that it would not be all that long before the Native Americans sought refuge over the border in Canada.

And of course he had been right, and even knowing it would happen sometime soon, it still came as a bit of shock to see the numbers of Sitting Bull's followers that it involved, when they discovered his very large camp.

Spotted Eagle, war chief of the Sans Arc Sioux, approached Walsh and told him that *"they were the first white men to dare approach Sitting Bull's camp so unconcernedly."* Walsh asked to meet Sitting Bull, which he did.

Public Domain Image
Commander James Morrow Walsh

Commander Walsh seemed to be a friendly man and asked why they had travelled to the White Mother's (Queen Victoria) country. Sitting Bull replied, *"To find peace."*

Public Domain Image

Sitting Bull explained that the Sioux had been persecuted by 'the blue-clad Long Knives,' and that they had been defending themselves for years. That they had constantly been forced to move on by the US soldiers who continued to occupy the Sioux hunting grounds, attacked the camps or villages without remorse killing many and destroying homes and food supplies. Constantly trying to force them to surrender.

Sitting Bull explained that their hope was that the White Mother, or Grandmother, (the term preferred by the Sioux), would give them sanctuary in her land.

Walsh explained to Sitting Bull that the Sioux were now on British soil and must abide by the White Mother's law. In simple terms the rules were applied to everyone in the territory equally, *"white man and red man alike"* and were enforced that way.

Making war against any other tribe there was against the law, as was stealing horses or anything else for that matter. And a huge no-no was using the White Mother's country and as a base to attack the US soldiers over the border.

Basically follow the rules and you can live here in peace for as long as you want. It would make a nice change for a Native American to hear such words. Sitting Bull agreed.

Sitting Bull liked what Walsh told him about the White Mother's laws, especially the same justice for all. He proudly showed Walsh the medals that King George III had given his grandfather for service to the British Crown during the War of 1812. (His grandfather had fought alongside the red-coated soldiers of the Shaganosh (British) king.) **"They were good men,"** Sitting Bull's grandfather had said, adding, **"If you should ever wish to find peace, go north to the land of redcoats."** Wikipedia

Being short of ammunition, Sitting Bull asked Walsh to supply them in order for them to be able to hunt buffalo. Walsh, who the Sioux had now called 'Long Lance' because of the red/white tipped lances the Mounties carried, agreed to supply the ammunition but only enough for hunting, and again reminded him of the White Mother's law. It was amicable and because of this Walsh and his men stayed in Sitting Bull's camp overnight.

Public Domain Image

A group of Canadian Mounties

Sadly the next morning, just as they were about to leave, three Assiniboines led by White Dog, were spotted returning to the camp with five horses which were recognised as belonging to a Roman Catholic priest living nearby. Walsh immediately arrested White Dog for theft. Not a good start to relationships.

Confused but quite confident that the Sioux warriors would not allow this white man to arrest him, turned quickly into surprise when no assistance came.

Walsh wanted to get to the bottom of the whole thing, as the law had so quickly been broken, and Walsh started to ask some very stern questions of White Dog by saying, **"*Tell me where you got these horses, how you got them, and what you intend doing with them, or I'll clap these irons on you and take you away.*"**

I think the Sioux were quite impressed with Walsh as he stood his ground and seemed quite adamant that he would carry out everything he said he would.

White Dog was on his own with this one and he knew it, so he a mumbled a response about seeing the horses wandering about loose and thought he could just take them. He hadn't realised that he had broken the law.

Walsh didn't believe him, but he gave him the benefit of the doubt. He took the horses away from White Dog and returned them to their owner. That was Walsh's resolve with all his Native Indians. Entering their camps, arresting those who had broken the White Mother's law, and never to showing any fear and being rather courageous under the circumstances. And this was something that the Sioux admired in anyone.

And by 1877 Walsh and his Mounties had a lot of policing to do with Sitting Bull's camp increasing steadily with approximately 4,000 camped there. But the Canadian Government were getting fidgety having so many Sioux on their land and wanted them out.

This feeling grew stronger as constant reports that Sitting Bull was building an army amongst the Native Americans within Canada with the intentions were to carry out widespread raiding.

Walsh and his Mounties investigated these stories but found them without any real truth, although the Native Canadian Blackfoot Chief Crow Foot agreed that Sitting Bull had approached him for support. But it was before the Battle of Little Big Horn so had nothing to do with the issue at hand.

Sitting Bull had been to see Crow Foot and the story is they got on very well considering being enemies to start with. This was a great time to be at peace with the Blackfoot Nation and Crowfoot, and it was decided by both parties that a meeting was a good idea. A powwow was arranged and the peace pipe used.

Public Domain Image

Crow Foot

Sitting Bull really liked Crowfoot. So much so that he named one of his sons after him.

Public Domain Image
Sitting Bull's son Crow Foot

But it wasn't all plain sailing between Walsh and Sitting Bull as they clashed many a time quite severely. But this didn't spoil their friendship for each other and it looked like Sitting Bull had actually found a white man that he could trust and respect. And it was mutual.

Walsh did feel that Sitting Bull had been 'grievously wronged' by the US Government and was not afraid to state this quite openly. He was named in newspapers of the day as 'Sitting Bull's Boss', and arranged a few interviews by the press for Sitting Bull to state his case.

Public Domain Image

Urged by Walsh to tell his own story to the world, Sitting Bull agreed to be interviewed by Stillson and Diehl, and the coverage went in to many an American newspaper. While Diehl interviewed, Stillson sketched Sitting Bull and the drawing appeared on the front of *Harper's Weekly* during December.

As to being 'Sitting Bull's Boss', Sitting Bull did seek Walsh's counsel and would adhere to his advice. If he felt it was the right advice for the Sioux that is.

But it wasn't a smooth and easy time. The vast presence of the Sioux in Canada had started to deplete the massive buffalo herds and between 1877-1881 they were almost hunted to extinction.

Everything seemed peaceful for the first year that Sitting Bull lived in Canada as meat and robes were plentiful making the winters there a bit easier. And the winters are notoriously cold in Canada, so food and clothing was very essential.

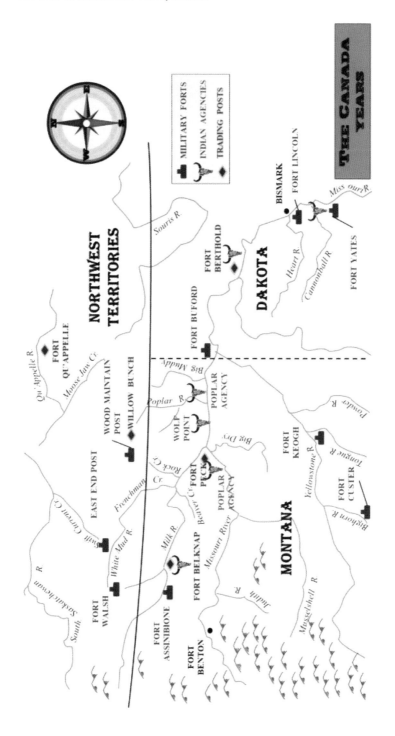

Trade was good for the Sioux. Trade with Jean Louis Legare at Wood Mountain and his trading post there. Legare was good to the Sioux, helping out on many occasions when they were near starvation, and trading goods with them as he was a fair man; he didn't try to cheat them as many other traders would have done.

LAST CONFERENCE OF JEAN LOUIS LEGARÉ AND SITTING BULL, 1881.

Public Domain Image
Jean Louis Legare Wood Mountain trading post

By 1878 Sitting Bull's camp had about 800 lodges including 45 lodges belonging to White Bird Nez Perces who had joined the Sioux. Also camped there were 240 lodges from Crazy Horse's band (Crazy Horse had since died), Little Hawk, Low Dog, and Black Fox of the Oglalas; Black Shield and Fools Heart of Miniconjous; Buffalo Hump of Sans Arc; Red Bear and Big Road. All very great leaders in their own right.

Public Domain Image **Little Hawk** Public Domain Image **Little Wolf** Public Domain Image **Red Cloud** Public Domain Image **White Bird**

Public Domain Image

Various Chiefs together

But the supply of buffalo dwindled causing unrest between Sitting Bull's tribes and the Canadian Natives already established there long before Sitting Bull arrived, and the competition for buffalo meat and hides increased just to survive. And naturally the Canadian Natives felt that it was all the fault of the Sioux that the buffalo had been depleted.

This discontent between the various tribes now residing in the area had the huge possibility of developing into clashes between them and there was only one solution. The Canadian Government decided that Sitting Bull and the Sioux had to go back to the US where they belonged.

The problem of Sitting Bull being in Canada also made relations between the US Government and the Canadian Government very difficult. And to complicate matters even further, London got involved. Well it was land belonging to Queen Victoria.

The US Government wanted assurances from the Canadian Government that Sitting Bull would not raid across the border. If they would not surrender, then Canada could keep them as refugees. I think in the hope that the Canadians would then create reservations for them on Canadian soil making them Canadian Natives and nothing to do with the US Government anymore. The Canadian Government resisted that idea quite forcibly.

In the meantime some of Sitting Bull's young warriors became eager to fight and hunt and ended up stealing a large amount of horses. The report of the stolen horses reached Walsh who immediately acted upon it, visiting Sitting Bull's camp, (Walsh lived very close by now in new headquarters there) and demanded the return of the horses. Or he would invite Colonel Miles into Canada to escort Sitting Bull back to the US. Sitting Bull was just a bit miffed at this, but returned the horses just in case.

Not long after, it's recorded that Sitting Bull called in to Walsh's camp as they were very short of supplies and demanded help. He said how unhappy he was that the White Mother had not provided as well as she should have done as far as provisions were concerned, and made various threats.

Walsh was annoyed and not prepared to sit and listen to Sitting Bull any longer. He said, *"Who do you think you are? Have you forgotten that you're American Indians? You haven't any right to be in Canada. You've caused our police any amount of trouble. You've stolen horses. You've been a goddamn nuisance. You seem to think all white men are afraid of you. Well, you're wrong. Get your goddamn provisions at the trading post. If you keep on making trouble, I'll put the whole damn lot of you in jail!"*

"Be careful, Wahonkeza (Walsh's Sioux name)," Sitting Bull replied, *"You're talking to the head of the mighty Sioux Nation."*

"I know who I'm talking to. What I said still stands. And if there's any more horse stealing, I'll put irons on you, too!"

Now Sitting Bull was angry and responded by saying, *"No man can talk to me like that!"*, and he reached for his gun, but Walsh grabbed him and threw him bodily out of his cabin. Sitting Bull landed rather ungainly apparently and in trying to get up Walsh gave him a swift kick in the behind.

Unable to contain his anger he again reached for his gun but this time one of the other Chiefs restrained him. There was a bit of a tussle but Sitting Bull calmed down and walked away.

But it didn't end there as Walsh called to his Mounties to prepare for a backlash from the Sioux over this and took unusual steps by asking for two poles to be placed on the ground at the fort. He then warned Sitting Bull and the Sioux that if they crossed over those poles. *"The first one who does will be sorry."*

Public Domain Image

Sitting Bull rode towards Walsh at speed. Then, just before he reached the poles, Sitting Bull stopped suddenly with the rest of the Sioux close behind him. Walsh and Sitting Bull just stared at each other. Then after what must have seemed like ages, Sitting Bull turned and rode off back to the camp.

Walsh was the only white man that had faced up to Sitting Bull in this way and I think Sitting Bull had a greater admiration for him then, even though he was extremely annoyed. After everything that had happened that day Walsh was still the only white man that Sitting Bull felt he could trust.

An embarrassing scene and a friendship tested to its limits.

But as the Canadian Government had made it very plain that they would not take on the responsibility of the Sioux, the US army kept on trying to bring Sitting Bull and the Sioux back to the US. Even offering Sitting Bull a pardon brought to him in Canada by Brigadier General Alfred H. Terry, (the man who had been part of the attack the Sioux at Little Big Horn), but only if Sitting Bull would return and settle on the reservation.

Public Domain Image

General Terry

Sitting Bull was persuaded to attend this meeting by Legare, and as a favour to Walsh, despite being in mourning for the death of his nine year old son.

General Terry was in attendance at this meeting and it was felt an insult to the Sioux as Terry had instructed Custer to attack the Sioux, then continued to persecute them and chase them into submission as retribution for Custer's death. He instigated the seizing of Sioux horses and guns and destroying their provisions in order to get them to surrender to the reservations. Having him there was a huge insult to the Sioux.

To repay the insult of Terry being at the meeting, the Sioux brought along a woman to speak. A huge no-no but to the Sioux it was payback time.

After much smoking of pipes, just to delay matters further, Terry explained that the Sioux would be treat with great respect. His comments were met with disdain. And more smoking.

Terry tried a more brusque approach and explained to Sitting Bull by saying, ***"This band of yours is the only one which has not surrendered. We have come hundreds of miles to bring you this message from the Great Father, who, as we have told you before, desires to live in peace with all his people. Too much white and***

Indian blood has already been shed. It is time that bloodshed should cease."

"What have we done that you should want us to stop?" asked Sitting Bull. *"We have done nothing. It is all the people on your side that have started us to do all these depredations. We could not go anywhere else, and so we took refuge in this country. I would like to know why you came here. You come here to tell us lies, but we don't want to hear them. I don't wish any such language used to me, to tell me such lies in my Great Mother's (Queen Victoria's) house. Don't say two more words. Go back home where you came from. The part of the country you gave me you ran me out of. I have now come here to stay with these people, and I intend to stay here."*

Other followers spoke only to reinforce Sitting Bull's words. The meeting was over and Terry knew it was hopeless trying to continue.

Sitting Bull sent him away.

He apparently said *"We did not give our country to you; you stole it. You come here to tell lies; when you go home, take them with you."*

The meeting was over.

This only helped to reinforce Commander Walsh remaining a supporter of Sitting Bull and the Sioux, and the two men remained firm friends, and peace reigned again in the region. With Walsh spending much of his command in the headquarters he had developed in Wood Mountain right in the heart of Sitting Bull's camp and his 5,000 followers.

But the peace didn't last for much longer as Walsh was then put into the very difficult situation by his superiors, of trying to persuade Sitting Bull to return to the US and surrender. But because of his friendship with Sitting Bull, the 'powers that be' decided that this was stopping Walsh from performing his duties as a commander there.

On July 13th 1880, because of this conflict of interest, Walsh was transferred to Fort Qu'Appelle, Saskatchewan, 140 miles away, where not long after that, he left for health reasons and returned to Ontario. He reluctantly resigned his commission three years later.

Sitting Bull was really sorry to be losing his great friend Walsh. As a parting gift and a mark of great respect, Sitting Bull presented Walsh with his eagle feather war bonnet and said, ***"Take this, my friend. I hope I never need it again. Every feather symbolizes a deed of courage when the Lakota were strong."*** It was a wonderful gesture and Walsh was proud to accept.

Not long after an Inspector Lief N. F. Crozier replaced him alongside a new commissioner Lieutenant Colonel Acheson G. Irvine. Both men took command and they both strived to rid Canada of the Sioux.

Public Domain Image
Lieutenant Colonel Acheson G. Irvine

Crozier would not act towards Sitting Bull as Walsh had done and refused to pay him any attention whatsoever. His aim was to destroy Sitting Bull's influence and standing within the tribe.

He approached other leaders and convinced them that the bloodshed had ceased now over the border and that it would be safe for them to return. Quite a few were convinced. But being near starvation had already helped their decision to surrender.

Spotted Eagle (Sans Arc Chief), a great follower of Sitting Bull left with 65 lodges and tribal members.

Public Domain Image
Rain in the Face

Soon after Rain in the Face (Hunkpapa) left with 15 lodges, and by October 31st 1880 had surrendered their horses and their arms to Bear Coat Miles.

By the end of 1880, 1510 Lakota and Cheyenne had surrendered.

Now Sitting Bull was left with only a few fighting men, women, children and old men too. He was undecided. What was the best move for his people?

They too were near starvation so he could understand that the promise of supplies from the US Government had helped Spotted Eagle and Rain in the Face to make that move. Sitting Bull wasn't as trusting.

Crozier and Irvine's tactic of splitting up the tribes was working. Those undecided leaders just had to look at their starving people and the promise of food and shelter must have sounded really good, despite it being a ploy.

Sitting Bull wanted to wait. He wanted to hear advice from his good friend Walsh who he felt would be returning soon. He did not know that Walsh had resigned. He had no trust for these white men who had never done anything to warrant his trust either, nor did they treat him with respect.

He could only see the reservation life being like a prison for the Sioux, and he envisaged his life to be spent in chains as he was blamed for Custer's death.

He puzzled over the fact that the US Government broke one of the Sioux cardinal rules of generosity as they refused to share their food. The Sioux would always share what they had if someone needed it more. Now the US Government were making the Sioux give up everything and literally making them beg for basic provisions.

So Sitting Bull and his people remained in Canada for four years, but the buffalo herds were much smaller here now which made hunting somewhat difficult and food in much shorter supply. Which also meant less hides for clothing and tipi repairs or replacements. Things were not looking good.

The Canadian Government would not take on the responsibility for the support and annuities for Sitting Bull and his people. Especially as there was a reservation waiting for them over the border. And the relationship between the Canadian Government and the US Government was becoming very fraught because of Sitting Bull's presence there.

Despite being originally made to feel welcome, it was still hard for the Sioux tribe living in Canada as the conditions were much harsher than what they were used to.

The Sioux started to suffer from starvation and disease and quite a few of them died sadly. Food shortages were unbelievable and they had resorted to eating mice when they could find them. They were malnourished, their clothing was tattered and they had nothing with which to repair their tipis. It was abject poverty and they almost froze to death in the harsh conditions there. It became a huge problem for Sitting Bull watching his family and his people starve before his eyes. And it could only lead to one thing.

And that was surrender to the US army which Sitting Bull did on July 19th 1881 and the start of reservation life.

Welcome to your new home.

SURRENDER AND RESERVATION

Surrender and Reservation

After a turbulent four years Sitting Bull had to move his people back to the US and surrender.

The buffalo were almost extinct now and he needed to find food as his people were starving. This only meant surrender to the white man and to join the reservation.

Sitting Bull arrived with nothing other than the shabby garments he was wearing. And the rest of the tribe didn't fare much better. Everything else had to be handed over to the US soldiers.

The surrender took place on July 19th 1881, when Sitting Bull and 186 of his people arrived at Fort Buford in Montana. His young son Crow Foot surrendered his Winchester lever–action carbine rifle to the commanding officer Major David H. Brotherton of Fort Buford, and Sitting Bull said that *"he hoped to teach the boy that he has become a friend of the Americans."*

FlintWestwood
https://commons.wikimedia.org/wiki/File:Fort_Buford_Barracks_2010.jpg
Fort Buford Barracks 2010, https://creativecommons.org/licenses/by-sa/3.0/legalcode
Reconstruction of Fort Burford

But he also added *"I wish it to be remembered that I was the last man of my tribe to surrender my rifle."*

To the Oglala Lakota's, Dakotas and Nakota, 'to surrender my rifle' means, **"We have killed enough white men with your own rifles so I give this rifle back to you, for Tunkasila Wakantanka (Grandfather Great Mystery) will use a different way to help us overcome the white man."**

At a surrender ceremony the next day in the Commanding Officer's Quarters, Sitting Bull told the four soldiers, twenty warriors and other guests in the small room that he **"wished to regard the soldiers and the white race as friends but he wanted to know who would teach his son the new ways of the world?"**

Public Domain Image
Sitting Bull and family

Sitting Bull was still a Chief and a holy man of the Hunkpapas and the Supreme Chief of the Lakota. The four cardinal virtues and the Sioux traditions still uppermost in his mind.

But sadly that had to change and Sitting Bull knew this. He had to change. For his people. All the Sioux were now confined to the reservation and the old way of living, their free life had now gone.

He had to take on this new mantle of guiding his people in the ways of the white man and learning to farm. It was the only way that he, their Chief, could protect his people from the white man and he would take any flak that came about. He had to be strong for the Sioux and remain a great leader.

Trying hard to secure some kind of rights for his people, Sitting Bull asked for permission to go back and forth into Canada whenever they wanted too. Plus a reservation of his own near the Black Hills. You can imagine how well received that was. But the US Government were still afraid of this legend and the power he held over his people.

Instead, as he posed this threat to all that was American, he was sent to Standing Rock Reservation. But even there the US Government were afraid that he would insight further fighting with the tribes already established there. To ensure that this didn't happen on August 26th 1881, Sitting Bull met with census taker William T. Selwyn who counted twelve people in Sitting Bull's immediate family and forty one other families in the tribe amounting to 195 people.

The US Government solution to the potential troubles they foresaw led them to transfer Sitting Bull and his people to Fort Yates before they were then taken further down the Missouri River to Fort Randall, where they were held as prisoners of war.

They travelled by steamboat (the General Sherman) down the Missouri River and spent the next 20 months there as prisoners. Once they had pitched their tipis, all 32 of them, close to Fort Randall itself, there was nothing left to do. Sitting Bull and his people just had to sit and vegetate eating army rations and putting up with becoming a curiosity for the white people to gawp at. Sitting Bull seemed resigned to his fate now, and had given up on any thoughts that his old life would return. His only way forward and that of the Sioux was to follow the white man's way.

He started to develop a financial mind and as many of the white onlookers were keen to have his autograph he happily charged for them and they happily paid. But his popularity did not instil any quick or positive decisions from the US Government regarding his return to Standing Rock and the rest of the tribe. They still could not decide how to deal with this man and his people.

They continued to be heavily guarded by US soldiers and even Colonel Andrews in charge there could not understand why they had been brought to the fort and not allowed to live with the rest of the tribe.

They didn't return to Standing Rock Reservation until May 10th 1883 where they joined the rest of their people there at long last.

Public Domain Image

The main control on reservations was held by agents. These agents had control over food/clothing, rations, the Indian Police and Indian Courts. They were tasked with pitting Chiefs against each other as a way to 'manage' the Indians. Holding back rations to gain further control then releasing rations once the Chief had complied with demands.

Public Domain Image
James McLaughlin

On the Great Sioux reservation was a man called James McLaughlin, the Indian Agent in charge of the reservation, or White Hair as he was called by the Sioux.

McLaughlin had taken on the role after working on other smaller agencies. He took his training as a United States Indian Agent and appeared to have good relationships with the Lakota on the reservation.

His role began at the Standing Rock Reservation, or the Great Sioux Reservation as it was originally known. He believed that his mission on the reservation was to encourage the Native Americans to assimilate into the white man's ways, disregard their traditions and cultures and learn to farm the land. Basically he was happy to 'destroy the culture of the Sioux and replace it with the white man's ideals'.

By now Sitting Bull's living conditions were so completely different to the nomadic ways he and his people had known for many, many moons. When Sitting Bull and his tribe arrived they were stripped of their weapons and their hard sought provisions and had to make do with the meagre offerings from the white man. They were starving and destitute. Their whole lifestyle had gone. The freedom they had had for centuries was now just a memory. They had no status, no traditions, and no life. Not anymore. But the anger was still there along with a sense of in justice. But his hands were tied to do anything about it.

And McLaughlin was determined that that was the way it would stay. He had no intention of allowing any special privileges to Chief Sitting Bull now in his care. He was just another Indian. Instead he made Sitting Bull work in the fields and generally tried to break his spirit and undermine any authority that Sitting Bull had with his tribe. McLaughlin treat him like an outcast, a nobody. He really thought that he could break the man.

McLaughlin in order to further humiliate Sitting Bull in the eyes of the Sioux tribe started to deal with Gall from the Hunkpapas and John Grass from the Blackfoot Sioux. Anything that he could do to show the Sioux that Sitting Bull had no influence there, he would do it.

Public Domain Image
John Grass

Public Domain Image
Chief Gall

But his tactics didn't work. Sitting Bull was too highly thought of by his tribe and by the numerous visitors, white men or Native Americans, that entered the reservation in the hope that they could meet Sitting Bull himself.

Sitting Bull tried hard to assert his tribal authority with McLaughlin only to be told that he was the same as anyone else on the reservation and would be treat the same too. Basically as far as McLaughlin was concerned Sitting Bull was just another Indian and he had to abide by the agency rules. Or else.

The dislike was mutual.

McLaughlin decided quickly that Sitting Bull was a trouble maker as Sitting Bull stood up against the white man's attempts at anything that he felt would be harmful to his people. But Sitting Bull did not try to stop his people from doing what he called the 'mindless work', meaning farming, if that's what they wanted to do. He was unhappy, that many seemed to have already forgotten the old ways already; he just wanted to protect his people and their traditions too.

What wasn't taken into account was that the land that the Sioux were expected to farm was totally wrong for any kind of farming, and the allotments given to them were far too small to do anything with.

In 1888 McLaughlin and other agents, plus a delegation from amongst the various Chiefs on the reservation travelled to meet with the Bureau of Indian Affairs (BIA) to discuss the Dawes Act.

Under the Sioux Act of 1888 the Great Sioux Reservation would be cut into six separate reservations: Pine Ridge, Rosebud, Cheyenne River, Standing Rock, Crow Creek, and Lower Brule. Each would gain enough land for its residents there.

The Dawes Act of 1887 (General Allotment Act) was simply another way to gain Native American lands. In simple terms and I quote, *"allows the President whenever he pleases to acquire Indians to give up their reservations for individual allotment."* This Act would affect a lot of tribes and on the Great Sioux Reservation would mean the loss of nine million acres of land.

© Mick Stothard 2020

Public Domain Image

This allowed the US Government to break up tribal lands by making them into individual plots. In effect making the Sioux give up their tribal land in exchange for a 'private parcel of land'. A parcel of land that was just enough for its occupants living there now. Sitting Bull was against this as he said that they would need all the land and more for their children and grandchildren. Good point.

"The objective of the Dawes Act was to assimilate Native Americans into mainstream US society by annihilating their cultural and social traditions." Wikipedia summary

It was decided that a meeting should be held in Washington to iron this problem out once and for all. Sitting Bull was one of the sixty one Chiefs taken along to this meeting on October 12th 1888. It caused a huge stir having so many 'savages' in one place like this. But it was a huge eye opener for the native contingent as they witnessed many 'wonders' of the white man's world while they were there.

One particular 'wonder' was the amazing paintings of Native Americans by an incredible artist called George Catlin. Paintings I have been very fortunate to be able to use as images in 'Comanche Life'. So I can understand their feeling of awe seeing Native Americans depicted so beautifully and life like as is Catlin's way with paints.

But they were also very impressed with The National Zoo never having seen such animals particularly the curious monkeys. What a time they must have had and the stories they had to tell when they returned.

But this slight deviation to amuse did not help the situation in hand. The US Government still wanted all the Sioux to become farmers and ranchers it was as simple as that. To become like the white man, forget your heritage your traditions, and live the right way, and give up 9 million acres of Sioux land so that they could sell this to white settlers for 50 cents per acre. It was a disaster for the Sioux but a success for the white man. Sitting Bull responded most forcefully to this new idea. But to no avail. It was a fabulous visit for Sitting Bull and the other leaders, but the trip didn't really help.

The Commissioners tasked with the breakup of the reservation lands tried to persuade the Sioux that Sitting Bull was trying to trick them or mislead them, and the offer was a huge benefit for the Sioux themselves.

But the Treaty of 1868 said that there had to be three quarters of Sioux signing the agreement and although twenty two Sioux signed and agreed. It still wasn't enough signatures to carry it through. So instead the Commissioners decided to ignore the treaty of 1868 and take the land without consent.

But the whole idea didn't sit well with a few in the US Government. So instead it became more of a threat to force them into selling by telling them that they would have the land taken away from them if they didn't sign. Sounds like the same deal to me.

As the Sioux trusted General George Crook, he was tasked with the duty to try and convince the Sioux of this good deal. But it was a heated meeting that went on for days and days. Despite what Crook was saying to the Sioux it always came out the same. We want your land.

White Hair McLaughlin was brought in to try and make the Sioux see sense, but Sitting Bull and the others were unmoved by the demands. He arranged further meetings but forgot to inform Sitting Bull that these meetings were taking place, even though he said that invites had gone out to all concerned. Sitting Bull was furious, but it was too late. The agreement was signed and the tribal lands had decreased even further for the advancement of the white man.

On leaving, a newspaperman approached Sitting Bull and asked how the 'Indians' felt about giving up their lands. Sitting Bull responded by saying, *"Indians? There are no Indians left but me."* The return to the reservation must have been a very unhappy one.

Sitting Bull's life on the reservation continued, and sadly continued to be a challenge too.

Living on the reservation for Sitting Bull meant a wooden cabin on the Grand River near to where he had been born. His life was free from fighting which was a good feeling and it meant that he had time to spend with his very large family. His two daughters by Snow on Her had presented him with grandchildren. One of his daughters, Many Horses, had married a man called Thomas Fly, and his youngest daughter, Walks Looking, married Andrew Fox had a son but died at the age of nineteen of a disease in 1887.

His home included two wives married in 1872 and five young children including two sets of twin boys and a daughter called Standing Holy born in 1878 whom he adored.

Crow Foot, his son (named after the Blackfoot Chief in Canada) and Sitting Bull were very close and continued so. But his extended family included friends and followers from the old days still remaining loyal and staying near to their great leader.

Sitting Bull's farm grew to consist of twenty horses, forty five cattle, eighty chickens and field of oats corn and potatoes. He built sheds and did well in his new life.

But every week, after a trip of 30 miles to the agency, he would collect his meat ration. This would be achieved from a large fenced off area (corral), and it would be announced which of the tribes turn it was to 'hunt' the 'steer' (ration cows). The animal, or if they were lucky animals, would then be released and 2-3 warriors, whooping and yelling, would either chase and kill the animal with their bows and arrows and sometimes pistols, or just shoot them as they stood at the fence. Once the animal was killed it would be skinned by the women, and divided up for everyone.

Even though Sitting Bull grew grains and vegetables, had cattle, lived in his log cabin and sent his children to the Congregational school, he was still openly disliked by McLaughlin.

Public Domain Image
A similar cabin to Sitting Bull's

But he still craved the old ways and the traditions he knew and loved and refused to conform to the white man's ways. Much to the displeasure of McLaughlin.

He was a holy man and would not give up his belief in the Great Spirit and become a Christian and despite the rules of the reservation being that only one wife was allowed, Sitting Bull rejected this too. He had five wives altogether. As far as religion was concerned, Sitting Bull understood that the white man could choose between being a Protestant or a Catholic. Why could the Sioux not choose too and continue believing in the Great Spirit? You can understand his reasoning here.

But he was keen to have his children educated in a nearby Christian school as he believed it was important for the next generation Sioux to be able to read and write.

There was even talk that Sitting Bull had been baptized into the Catholic Church and Indian Agent McLaughlin was very quick to scotch these rumours as rubbish saying *"There is no immediate prospect of such ceremony so far as I am aware."*

Sitting Bull was to have another of his visions but this time it foretold something much more sinister.

Public Domain Image

This time he saw a meadowlark land on a hillock beside him, and he heard it speaking to him saying, *"Your own people, Lakotas, will kill you."* Nearly five years later, this vision also proved to be true.

RAILWAY SPEECH

Public Domain Image

Railway speech

By the time Sitting Bull and his tribe had returned to the US from Canada, a lot of the land had become railroad land and the railway was almost complete.

The railroads had a new money making idea which was rail tours of buffalo territory giving their tourists the opportunity to shoot the animals from the comfort of the train. As a result, the buffalo numbers started to dwindle.

Public Domain Image

With this new venture, as well as the arrival of the very enthusiastic buffalo hunters who could shoot and kill hundreds of the animals, have them skinned, and packed off to the tanning factories, the animals became an endangered species. And the Native Americans starved, while the white man made a fortune.

Public Domain Image

About four million buffalo were killed just for their fur and their bones; just slaughtered and left to rot. Later the bones were collected and sold as fertilizer making further profit for the white man.

Public Domain Image

Hunters were paid a bounty to kill as many buffalo as possible. Massive great piles of buffalo skulls were seen everywhere on the prairies of the Dakotas and Montana. And many buffalo hunters became famous such as, Brick Bond (they had some very unusual names) a legend in buffalo hunting, who was working for the railroad as a hunter. He reportedly killed 250 animals a day. Also a renowned hunter called Tom Nixon is reported to have shot 120 animals in 40 minutes. He continued his 'record' in 1873 when he slaughtered 3,200 in 35 days, which beat Buffalo Bill Cody's record of killing 4,280 in 18 months making his record pale in comparison.

The demand for buffalo meat continued just to feed the railway workers building the railroad in the 1860s. Buffalo Bill Cody was hired by the railroad for this purpose. Buffalo Bill earned about $500 a month (about $11,624 today).

But it was all done for a purpose. Yes to make a huge amount of money, but it was also felt that it was *"Better [to] kill the buffalo than have him feed the Sioux."* They wanted to break the Sioux and get them to conform and force them to live on hand-outs from the government.

Public Domain Image

Because of this it was decided that it would be a great idea to have Chief Sitting Bull at the railroad completion celebration and make a speech. On September 8th 1883, that's exactly what he did.

Sitting Bull spoke in front of government officials, railroad barons, and the US military in honour of the completion of the Northern Pacific Railway.

Public Domain Image

It was a huge ceremony where the two ends of the rail lines met with the final rail spike (gold spike) hammered into place.

Guests of honour included "President Ulysses S. Grant, Secretary of State Henry Teller, the governors of every state that the railway connected, Northern Pacific president Henry Villard, and the bankers and investors who would rake in the profits from their venture. Other guests included diplomats from Germany, Great Britain and the Netherlands. Plus the defeated leader of the Sioux Nation, Sitting Bull, who had submitted a draft of his speech in advance for approval."

Sitting Bull had the honour to ride at the head of the ceremonial parade. Along with his army chaperone that is.

Sitting Bull's speech, written with help and suggestions from a young army officer who spoke Sioux, was delivered in his Sioux language. Much to the surprise of the vast audience. But they would have got a bigger surprise if they had understood when he said, *"I hate all White people,"* he said. *"You are thieves and liars. You have taken away our land and made us outcasts."*

Public Domain Image

This gave him the opportunity of expressing his opinion to those that had made him and his peoples life so difficult losing out in the end and having to surrender despite his continuous battles against them.

Sitting Bull continued in this vane as he described all the cruelty the Sioux nation had endured at the hands of the United States. Occasionally he would pause for breath and the audience would clap under the impression that he was saying something complimentary about the railroad.

They would clap, he would bow, then he would continue his description of the white man's 'corruption and dishonesty'. All in his Sioux language.

At this time you have to feel sorry for the young army officer who had spent time with Sitting Bull getting the speech just right, and now he knew it was pointless trying to stop him. Nor would it have been any good translating it either.

Once Sitting Bull ended his speech, he received a standing ovation. They loved him. If only they had known.

Public Domain Image

Buffalo Bill was rather impressed with Sitting Bull and requested that he be allowed to tour with the show.

In order to try to reduce the problems that McLaughlin felt Sitting Bull was causing on the reservation, and to get rid of him too, McLaughlin allowed Sitting Bull to join Buffalo Bill's Wild West Show.

BUFFALO BILL'S WILD WEST SHOW

Public Domain Image

Buffalo Bill's Wild West Show

   How exciting it must have been for all those ticket holders to watch the spectacle of Buffalo Bill's Wild West Show. To be there and to watch those 'savages' getting their comeuppance at last.

But the whole idea proved very lucrative for Buffalo Bill Cody.

Public Domain Image
Buffalo Bill

They were basically travelling vaudeville shows starting around the 1870s up until the whole idea waned in the 1920s. They gave a completely different look at what the cowboys and the Plains Indians were actually like during the exciting times of the America West. Rose tinted glasses I think the term is, as they sensationalised the whole concept of the Wild West. But they were loved and extremely popular.

The storyline and even some of the characters did or had existed, but the Native American was always portrayed as the 'bad guy'. And got many a hefty 'booooo' from the crowds for their trouble.

The fascination and interest for more stories and details of the Wild West really started with the very cheap 'dime novels'. The Wild West was an exciting place and people wanted to read about it, even if it was all made up. Didn't make any difference and they sold like hot cakes.

A guy called Ned Buntline wrote a novel about one particular hero in 1869, a buffalo hunter, US Army scout and also a guide. This man was called William F. Buffalo Bill Cody and the novel was *called **Buffalo Bill, the King of Border Men***. Buntline had met Buffalo Bill on a train and was fascinated by his life, hence the novel. And Buffalo Bill's notoriety began.

Public Domain Image

Buffalo Bill's Wild West Show was a huge success wherever it went. So successful that it toured Europe eight times between 1887 and 1892 with the last tours happening in 1902 to 1906. The first tour became part of the American Exhibition with the Golden Jubilee of Queen Victoria.

The shows were lengthy affairs lasting about 3-4 hours. But with marvellous displays of sharpshooting, hunts, races, rodeo events, they were worth the long sit down for the thousands that attended.

After a parade on horseback to start the show, massive battle re-enactments would be the norm, with a buffalo hunt, a train robbery and of course those pesky Indians at war.

But the finale must have been a sight to see as it was usually based on an Indian attack on a white settlers burning cabin, with the Indians being seen off by Buffalo Bill and his cowboys.

Re-enactments were lavish events. Buffalo Bill included something historical such as the "Battle of Little Big Horn" or "Custer's Last Stand". A man named Buck Taylor played the part of Custer and when the battle is over and Custer and all his men lay dead on the ground of the arena, who should ride in but our hero Buffalo Bill. But he's too late to save Custer. So he wreaks revenge by killing and scalping Yellow Hand and called it 'the first scalp for Custer'.

Public Domain Image

All good family stuff. And it didn't stop there. There were shooting competitions and skill was shown in the many displays of marksmanship. Annie Oakley being a major part of this, with her talent with guns and rifles.

ANNIE OAKLEY.
Famous Rifle Shot and Holder of the Police Gazette Championship Medal

Public Domain Image
Annie Oakley

Women did play a part in the shows and were a big attraction too. Annie being a very popular lady, starring in the show for sixteen years, with her sharpshooting and billing of "Miss Annie Oakley, the Peerless Lady Wing-Shot".

Calamity Jane was another popular woman performer, being famous as a notorious frontierswoman who was the subject of many wild stories, many she made up herself, but they probably made better stories that way. In the show, she was a skilled horsewoman and expert rifle and revolver handler. But sadly this ended in 1902, when she was reportedly sacked from the show for drinking and fighting.

Many animals took part to entertain particularly in the rodeo events with the broncos (unbroken horses) throwing or bucking their riders from their backs to the amazement of the crowds.

Races were another form of entertainment employed in the Wild West show. Running races between ponies and Indian runners, Sioux boys bareback riding and even lady riders racing each other. All very exciting to watch no doubt.

This was also somewhere for you to see your heroes in action too, and many a famous name would be part of Buffalo Bill's show. Stars like Will Rogers, Tom Mix and some unusual ones like Bill Pickett, Pawnee Bill and Johnny Baker who was the 'Cowboy Kid', Mexican Joe, Bronco Bill and Coyote Bill. Sometimes the show would have had around 1,200 performers just for one show. Fascinating and a nightmare to organise successfully I would have thought. But they went very well.

I don't think the show would have been as popular if it hadn't been for the token actors taken from the Native Americans such as the Lakota people.

They were hired to be part of the staged "Indian Races" and obviously in the battles they were told to act out "savagery and wildness" against the white settlers also in the show. This depicted them as the cruel savage beasts that the white man felt that they already were. They were given clothing that had nothing to do with what they would have worn and even the native women were dressed in a warriors apparel with breastplate and headdresses, and cheeky little leather shorts which must have been quite embarrassing for them. But the crowd would have loved it.

The Lakota Sioux Ghost Dance was a popular performance and it fed the audiences imagination of weird traditions and cruelty that the Native American 'savages' did as the norm.

One of the big stars to perform happened in 1884 when reservation Indian Agent McLaughlin was approached by show promoter Alvaren Allen, asking if Sitting Bull would be allowed to leave the reservation and join Buffalo Bill's Wild West Show. The show would tour parts of the northern US and Canada, and the show was to be called the '*Sitting Bull Connection*'.

Public Domain Image

Public Domain Image

Fancy that. Having a really famous and notorious Plains Indian there in the arena for all to see. McLaughlin agreed and Sitting Bull started a new phase in his life.

Sitting Bull earned about $50 a week (about $1,423 today) and rode around the arena so that the audience could get a good look at him. He was very popular, even though it is said that as he rode around the arena he would shout unpleasant things to the audience in his language. And they lapped it all up. Although some heckled and booed when he was on. But this didn't stop him performing. He was a celebrity and many white men wanted to see *"the Slayer of General Custer"*.

Mind you historians argue about this as some say he made speeches about his wish for better education and how he wished for better relationships between the Sioux and the white man. Who knows? Perhaps the actual translation wasn't all that good. It wouldn't be the first time he had said something rather profound.

But he stayed with the show for four months before returning back to the reservation. The audiences loved him and as far as they were concerned he was a star and a warrior. He even met President Grover Cleveland and he felt that was right as after all he was a Chief too.

But being the man he was he often gave his money away to any homeless people he encountered or just beggars in the street of the cities he visited, and he could not understand how there was so much poverty amongst all the wealth in the US.

He became great friends with not only Buffalo Bill himself but Annie Oakley too. Sitting Bull met Annie Oakley during the tour and was very impressed by her sharpshooting skills. So impressed that he offered $65 (about $1,850 today), just to have a photo taken with them both together.

The friendship, admiration and respect went both ways, as Oakley apparently said that Sitting Bull made a 'great pet' of her. I think she meant that he was protective and cared for her, which is rather nice.

She was only five feet tall and he named her affectionately "Watanya Cicilla" meaning 'Little Sure Shot' which became her trademark name in adverts for the show. What she lacked in height she gained on stage as an exceptionally talented marksman, and a caring individual of other performers.

Sitting Bull and Annie Oakley

Sitting Bull felt that her sharpshooting talent was a gift given to her by supernatural forces, which he strongly believed in. His respect and admiration was so strong that in 1884 he 'adopted' her as his daughter. High esteem indeed.

Other familiar Native Americans names who performed in the show were Red Cloud, Chief Joseph, Geronimo, and the Modoc War scout Donald McKay.

Sitting Bull and Buffalo Bill

GHOST DANCE

Public Domain Image

Ghost Dance

Sitting Bull's time with Buffalo Bill's Wild West Show came to an end, but even with his time away from the reservation Indian Agent McLaughlin still felt uneasy having him around again. McLaughlin saw Sitting Bull as a trouble maker and was determined to stamp down on him hard. Because of this, tensions were high between both of them and the disputes over the sale of some of the Great Sioux Reservation didn't help the situation.

Sitting Bull had tried, to no avail, to stop the US Government selling off more and more of the reservation lands. His efforts were fruitless and the lands was sold to even more white settlers, and the Sioux had to try and scrape a living on the almost barren lands left to them.

During this time an Indian Rights Activist named Caroline Weldon arrived at the reservation from Brooklyn New York. She was a member of the National Indian Defence Association (NIDA) and was keen to assist Sitting Bull as his secretary, 'voice' (interpreter) and supporter, and resolved to devote her life to the welfare of the Sioux.

Weldon took the amazing step of joining the Sioux and living on the reservation with her young son Christy, living in very close quarters with Sitting Bull and his family. Her intention had been to start an 'Indian' school at Sitting Bull's camp, but this was strongly opposed by McLaughlin.

She may have had a good working relationship with Sitting Bull, but her actions and her confrontational attitude towards Indian Agent McLaughlin did not help a great deal. Nor did it help her 'public face' as McLaughlin started a 'smear campaign' against her which increased the ill feeling the white community on the reservation and beyond had for her and the press slated her at every opportunity. The press called her "Sitting Bull's White Squaw" and this slanderous description of her led her to the only option she had left, and that was to leave.

Despite the vilification, Weldon did try to warn Sitting Bull that the Ghost Dance Movement would bring nothing but trouble to his doorstep, as it gave the US Government the perfect reason for the military to step in and destroy him and the Sioux Nation.

The smear campaign against her and with Sitting Bull sticking to his guns, helped to end the relationship between Sitting Bull and Weldon, and she left the reservation. Sadly her words came true later.

And the Ghost Dance arrived on the reservation during a time of great hardship due to the very harsh winters on the reservation. Word of it had already reached Pine Ridge, Rosebud and Cheyenne River reservations, and the leaders sent out representatives to try and find out more about this new religion.

It all revolved around a Paiute Indian named Wovoka, (also known as prophet Jack Wilson), who had started a new religious movement that spread like wild fire amongst the Plains Indians culminating on the reservations themselves, as Paiute had had a vision that Jesus Christ, had returned to Earth in the form of a Native American. Quite a vision.

Public Domain Image
Paiute Indian named Wovoka

He was preaching a kind of mix of Indian beliefs and Christian teachings too. And by performing the 'Ghost Dance', Indians would live forever in a land that was free of the white man, full of different game for them to hunt, no sickness or hunger, peace at last, and all their generations of ancestors would be there waiting for them.

Many were keen to listen to his words and early in the 1890s Kicking Bear, a Miniconjou Lakota after attending one of Wovoka speeches reported back with a message saying, *"the earth had grown old and tired. The Messiah would cover it with a deep new layer of soil. Sweet grass, running water, and trees would adorn the surface, while herds of ponies, buffalo and other game would wander in abundance – that my red children may eat and drink, hunt and rejoice."*

Public Domain Image
Kicking Bear

Sitting Bull was not convinced.

The Ghost Dance Movement, as it was called, required the tribes to dance and chant to help their deceased relatives rise from the dead, and herald the return of the buffalo. And the dance was performed slow and solemn as a shuffle in silence to a slow, single drumbeat. A dancing ceremony, that would rid the Native American land of white people, so that Native Americans could establish themselves back into their traditions and way of life again. It would be like a dream come true for them.

The dance included wearing shirts that had magical powers and could stop any of the white man's bullets from penetrating and harming the wearer. Or so they believed.

Sioux in the Pine Ridge and Rosebud Reservations had already started doing the Ghost Dance much to the discomfort of the Indian Agents there who had already asked for help from the army to 'nip this in the bud'.

Because of the unrest that had been caused in the other reservations over the Ghost Dance, many soldiers had arrived and were literally on 'stand by' just in case they were needed. They did not feel that they should just steam in and put a stop to it but hoped that their presence might just halt things.

Newspapers had already homed in on the reservations to report on the terrible 'savage' dance and the crazed new religion that had stirred the Sioux into a frenzy. At Standing Rock, the authorities feared that Sitting Bull, still revered as a spiritual leader, would join the Ghost Dancers as well. McLaughlin did not want this kind of publicity at his reservation. Not if he could help it.

Public Domain Image
Rev Mary Collins

Living at the reservation was a missionary called Rev. Mary Collins. She had been living and working with the Sioux for about 35 years, spoke the language very well and was well respected by the Sioux. Her knowledge of medicine gave her a high status within the tribe, and she was happy to counsel on domestic issues, religious matters and any legality they may have had.

She acted as a teacher, translator, and a liaison between the Sioux and the white man, and was a very good friend of Sitting Bull. She shared her vast knowledge and experience of the Sioux and the Native American lifestyle with many universities, public schools, churches and at various conferences too. She was definitely a champion for the Native American and a great supporter of the Sioux.

But the word and the dance spread to the Standing Rock Agency and Sitting Bull allowed the dancers to congregate in his camp. The whole concept of the dance had become hugely popular with the Sioux.

Although he himself did not participate in the dance it was still Sitting Bull who was blamed for the excited interest on the reservation.

Rev. Collins tried to use her close relationship with Sitting Bull to try and persuade him not to encourage the Ghost Dance any further. To maintain peace and harmony with the white man and to encourage his people to go back to their farms as they had been neglecting them. This didn't help.

As the tribe's spiritual leader, the white men at the reservation, McLaughlin included, could only see Sitting Bull condoning and encouraging such a movement. The panic started to set in with the white settlements nearby, and even the US army started to get fidgety as they didn't understand what was happening nor did they care. They just saw trouble brewing.

As the tension between Sitting Bull and Indian Agent McLaughlin had never been good, McLaughlin's first instinct was to order the arrest of Sitting Bull before he became fully involved and instigated a fully fledged riot and also try to escape from the reservation. Or at least that is what McLaughlin had decided was going to happen.

So McLaughlin sent in the Indian Police to arrest Sitting Bull. This was December 15th 1890 and it turned out to be a day long remembered but as a very bad day for many. The Sioux particularly.

DEATH

Flickr: Commercial Use Allowed

Death

Indian Agent James McLaughlin, under the impression that Sitting Bull was planning to escape from the reservation with the Ghost Dancers, ordered the Indian Police to arrest him.

With this already fixed in his mind, McLaughlin had written to Lieutenant Henry Bullhead who was an Indian Agency Policeman. The letter gave detailed instructions as to how to handle the arrest and capture of Sitting Bull at dawn on December 15th 1890, and to use a light spring wagon. All of this to happen quietly and before the rest of Sitting Bull's tribe had awoken.

Public Domain Image

The wagon idea was abandoned by Lieutenant Bullhead, as a quicker get away would be to put Sitting Bull onto his horse, (the horse given to him by Buffalo Bill some years ago), straight after the arrest. Well you and I know the best laid plans never come to fruition.

Public Domain Image

Just before dawn broke, 39 police officers and four volunteers (Special Constables sworn in for this task wearing white handkerchiefs around their necks to distinguish them from the others), arrived at Sitting Bull's cabin. The Police were mostly made up of Lakota Sioux men themselves. At various points some of the police officers surrounded the cabin, whilst others barged in.

Sitting Bull was informed by Bullhead of his arrest. In order to stall for a bit of time Sitting Bull and his wife complained bitterly and loudly successfully waking the camp who converged on Sitting Bull's cabin. Sitting Bull was dragged unceremoniously outside.

Bullhead told Sitting Bull that the Indian agent needed to speak with him and he needed to come with them on horseback. Once the meeting was over he could return to his cabin and family. No problems.

Sitting Bull refused to oblige, and the Indian Police started to resort to force. This angered the tribal members congregating outside the cabin. So much so that tribal members gathered to try and protect him, but it just got very messy. Sitting Bull still standing firm, refused to cooperate with the Indian Police and a scuffle started.

Public Domain Image

Red Tomahawk

Catch-the-Bear, a Lakota Sioux, aimed his rifle and shot Bullhead in his side, who reacted as he fell by shooting Sitting Bull in the chest with his revolver. Another police officer, Red Tomahawk, reacted really badly by shooting Sitting Bull in the back of his head, and Sitting Bull dropped to the ground. The great spiritual leader Sitting Bull died immediately on December 15th 1890.

This started a vicious battle as furious Sioux attacked the Indian Police with guns, knives and clubs. Anything they could get their hands on.

Sitting Bull dying this way infuriated the tribe and the fight continued with several men losing their lives. The Sioux killed six of the policemen on the spot, but two others died shortly afterwards. Bullhead included after many more bullets were shot into his body. The Indian police however succeeded in killing seven of the tribe, two of their horses and of course Sitting Bull himself. It only took a few minutes but many died or were wounded that day. And a great leader was lost.

Public Domain Image

This telegram was sent out after Sitting Bull's death stating that **"Squaws death chant heard in every direction,"** The great man was being mourned and it must have been a fearful sound for the white man.

His death led many of the Sioux to leave the reservation rather quickly to save any further deaths, particularly theirs, from the soldiers there.

Public Domain Image
Sitting Bull's grave at Fort Yates, 1906

Sitting Bull's body was placed in an army made coffin and buried in Fort Yates Military Cemetery in North Dakota by the army on December 17th without any ceremony at all. As a 'pagan' he was not allowed a Christian burial. This was what we would call a 'paupers grave'.

In 1953, his family exhumed what they believed to be his remains, and re-buried him near Mobridge South Dakota, near his birthplace. When his body was removed from the original grave, a monument was place as a marker there.

Public Domain Image
Monument at Sitting Bull's grave, Mobridge, South Dakota, 2003

But there is no guarantee that Sitting Bull rests easy as there is a possibility that he may (or may not) be resting in differing grave sites.

Perhaps he still rests at Fort Yates where he was buried in December 1890.

Or he could be resting at Mobridge South Dakota where a monument stands in his honour.

Or he is in both sites literally, his bones split between North Dakota and South Dakota as it is said that his grave was opened a few times between 1890 and 1953. Or perhaps his bones lie somewhere unmarked, but situated somewhere within the land he loved.

Whatever happened to Sitting Bull, he will always be remembered among the Lakota Sioux, the Hunkpapas, not only as *"an inspirational leader and fearless warrior but as a loving father, a gifted singer, a man always affable and friendly toward others, whose deep religious faith gave him prophetic insight and lent special power to his prayers."*

A former Indian agent Valentine T. McGillycuddy from the Pine Ridge Reservation was asked his opinion on the "hostilities" surrounding the Ghost Dance movement, by General Leonard Wright Colby, commander of the Nebraska National Guard (portion of letter dated January 15, 1891). This is his response.

"As for the 'Ghost Dance' too much attention has been paid to it. It was only the symptom or surface indication of a deep rooted, long existing difficulty; as well treat the eruption of small pox as the disease and ignore the constitutional disease.

As regards disarming the Sioux, however desirable it may appear, I consider it neither advisable, nor practicable. I fear it will result as the theoretical enforcement of prohibition in Kansas, Iowa and Dakota; you will succeed in disarming and keeping disarmed the friendly Indians because you can, and you will not succeed with the mob element because you cannot.

If I were again to be an Indian agent, and had my choice, I would take charge of 10,000 armed Sioux in preference to a like number of disarmed ones; and furthermore agree to handle that number, or the whole Sioux nation, without a white soldier. Respectfully, etc., V.T. McGillycuddy.

P.S. I neglected to state that up to date there has been neither a Sioux outbreak or war. No citizen in Nebraska or Dakota has been killed, molested or can show the scratch of a pin, and no property has been destroyed off the reservation."

Sitting Bull's friend, James M. Walsh, after hearing about the death is reported to have said, *"I am glad to learn that Bull is relieved of his miseries even if it took the bullet to do it. A man who wields such power as Bull once did, that of a King, over a wild spirited people cannot endure abject poverty slavery and beggary without suffering great mental pain and death is a relief. Bull's confidence and belief in the Great Spirit was stronger than I ever saw in any other man. He trusted to him implicitly. History does not tell us that a greater Indian than Bull ever lived, he was the Mohommat of his people the law the King maker of the Sioux."*

Two weeks later the massacre at Wounded Knee would take place.

WOUNDED KNEE MASSACRE

Public Domain Image

Wounded Knee Massacre

The massacre of several hundred Sioux has now become famous in history as the *Wounded Knee Massacre* or the *Battle of Wounded Knee.*

It happened about two weeks after Sitting Bull's death on December 29th 1890 near Wounded Knee Creek on the Lakota Pine Ridge Indian Reservation, South Dakota.

US Army Arrives

A troop of the US 7th Cavalry led by Major Samuel M. Whitside stopped Spotted Elk's band of Miniconjou and thirty eight Hunkpapa Lakota near Porcupine Butte, as they were trying to escape from the reservation after Sitting Bull's death fearing repercussions. The US 7th Cavalry escorted them to Wounded Knee Creek about five miles further on, and they were advised to make camp there.

The rest of the cavalry, led by Colonel James W. Forsyth, arrived and surrounded the whole of the camp with the peaceful gesture of having four Hotchkiss mountain guns with them.

Public Domain Image

On the morning of December 29th, the US Cavalry troops entered the camp with the aim of disarming the tribes and it went very badly wrong.

Several variations on the same theme have been recorded on how the events of the massacre occurred. One of the versions states that a US Cavalry soldier tried to disarm a deaf tribesman called Black Coyote, who for obvious reasons, did not understand why the soldier was trying to take his rifle. The rifle had cost him a lot, and he didn't want to just hand it over to a stranger. Sadly in the scuffle, it went off accidentally and the shooting commenced.

Another version states that an old tribesman was performing the Ghost Dance. Black Coyote's rifle went off and the US army began shooting at the Sioux. The warriors fought back, but many had already been given up their weapons and didn't stand a chance.

It all happened so quickly and at close range that many warriors were killed or wounded before they had a chance to retaliate. Some managed to re-claim their rifles and fire back but as they had nowhere to hide and gain any cover, they were picked off quickly.

The soldiers brought in the Hotchkiss guns and managed to decimate the tipis and the occupants with their deadly fire. Admittedly with it being such close range, quite a few soldiers lost their lives to 'friendly fire'.

Public Domain Image

Hotchkiss mountain guns

Some of the women and children managed to flee the camp and hide from the shooting, but there was only blood lust now and the soldiers decided to spread out and finish off any wounded tribesmen.

More soldiers used horses to pursue the fleeing women and children, quite often for miles just to make sure that they finished them off too.

Public Domain Image

When the shooting had stopped over, *"250 men, women, and children of the Lakota had been killed and 51 were wounded (4 men and 47 women and children, some of whom died later); some estimates placed the number of dead as high as 300.*

Twenty-five soldiers also died, and thirty-nine were wounded (six of the wounded later died).

Twenty soldiers were awarded the Medal of Honour. In 2001, the National Congress of American Indians passed two resolutions condemning the military awards and called on the US government to rescind them. The Wounded Knee Battlefield, site of the massacre, has been designated a National Historic Landmark by the US Department of the Interior. In 1990, both houses of the US Congress passed a resolution on the historical centennial formally expressing 'deep regret' for the massacre."   Wikipedia

WITNESS STATEMENTS

Thomas Tibbles (1840–1928); journalist:

"Suddenly, I heard a single shot from the direction of the troops. Then three or four. A few more. And immediately, a volley. At once came a general rattle of rifle firing then the Hotchkiss guns."

Black Elk (1863–1950); medicine man, Oglala Lakota:

"I did not know then how much was ended. When I look back now from this high hill of my old age, I can still see the butchered women and children lying heaped and scattered all along the crooked gulch as plain as when I saw them with eyes still young. And I can see that something else died there in the bloody mud, and was buried in the blizzard. A people's dream died there. It was a beautiful dream. And I, to whom so great a vision was given in my youth, — you see me now a pitiful old man who has done nothing, for the nation's hoop is broken and scattered. There is no centre any longer, and the sacred tree is dead."

American Horse (1840–1908); Chief, Oglala Lakota:

"There was a woman with an infant in her arms who was killed as she almost touched the flag of truce ... A mother was shot down with her infant; the child not knowing that its mother was dead was still nursing ... The women as they were fleeing with their babies were killed together, shot right through ... and after most all of them had been killed a cry was made that all those who were not killed or wounded should come forth and they would be safe. Little boys ... came out of their places of refuge, and as soon as they came in sight a number of soldiers surrounded them and butchered them there."

Edward S. Godfrey; Captain, commanded Company 'D' of the 7th Cavalry:

"I know the men did not aim deliberately and they were greatly excited. I don't believe they saw their sights. They fired rapidly but it seemed to me only a few seconds till there was not a living thing before us; warriors, squaws, children, ponies, and dogs ... went down before that unaimed fire." (Godfrey was a lieutenant in Captain Benteen's force during the Battle of the Little Bighorn.)

Public Domain Image

Dead Medicine Man

Public Domain Image

Public Domain Image

Frozen bodies

Three days later, after a very bad blizzard, the military hired civilians to deal with the dead at Wounded Knee.

Public Domain Image

Hired civilians

What they found would live with them forever as the dead had frozen where they had died.

Public Domain Image

Once they had gathered the frozen bodies, for which they were paid $2 per body, the bodies were then interred in a mass grave on a hill overlooking where the camp had been, and exactly on the spot from where the Hotchkiss guns had been placed to fire on the Sioux.

Public Domain Image

Mass Grave

History states that four infants were found alive amongst the dead. What happened to them I cannot tell you.

The mass grave held 84 men, 44 women and 18 children.

Colonel Forsyth was relieved of command, and an Army Court of Inquiry began. But despite everything that had happened, Forsyth was reinstated as Colonel of the 7th Cavalry.

Public Domain Image
Colonel Nelson A. Miles

Public Domain Image
Colonel Forsyth

Miles criticised Forsyth as he felt that Forsyth had deliberately disobeyed his orders so that he could destroy the Sioux. That Wounded Knee was a *"deliberate massacre rather than a tragedy caused by poor decisions"*. Miles really wanted to ruin Forsyth's career but failed completely when the whole affair was whitewashed and Forsyth was promoted to Major General.

Not long after the massacre a man called Dewey Beard, his brother Joseph Horn Cloud, who survived the massacre, with others formed the Wounded Knee Survivors Association which came to include massacre descendants.

Compensation was requested from the US Government for the many deaths at the massacre site, and to this day the association works independently to *"preserve and protect the historic site from exploitation, and to administer any memorial erected there"*.

It was not until the 1990s that a memorial to the Lakota was included in the National Historic Landmark.

Public Domain Image
Brothers, (left to right) White Lance, Joseph Horn Cloud, and Dewey Beard, Wounded Knee survivors; Miniconjou

"Historically, Wounded Knee is generally considered to be the end of the collective multi-century series of conflicts between colonial and US forces and American Indians, known collectively as the Indian Wars. It was not however the last armed conflict between Native Americans and the United States."

LEGACY/MEMORIALS

Public Domain Image

Legacy/Memorials

➤ Following Sitting Bull's death, his cabin on the Grand River was taken to Chicago for use as an exhibit at the 1893 World's Columbian Exposition. Native American dancers also performed at the Exposition.

➤ On September 14th 1989, the United States Postal Service released a Great Americans series 28¢ postage stamp featuring a likeness of Sitting Bull.

➤ On March 6th 1996, Standing Rock College was renamed Sitting Bull College in his honour. Sitting Bull College serves as an institution of higher education on Sitting Bull's home of Standing Rock in North Dakota and South Dakota.

➤ The American historian Gary Clayton Anderson of the University of Oklahoma published Sitting Bull and the Paradox of Lakota Nationhood (2010), a revisionist examination of the Lakota medicine man. Anderson stresses the Little Big Horn in light of past successes of the Lakota Nation and the merits of Sitting Bull himself, rather than simply a mishap by Custer.

➤ In August 2010, a research team led by Eske Willerslev, an ancient DNA expert at the University of Copenhagen, announced their intention to sequence the genome (an entire set of genes) of Sitting Bull, with the approval of his descendants, using a hair sample obtained during his lifetime.

Both inside and outside the reservation boundaries in West River, the Lakota are an integral part of the region and its history: many towns have Lakota names, such as Owanka, Wasta, and Oacoma. Towns such as Hot Springs, Timber Lake, and Spearfish are named in English after the original Lakota names. Some rivers and mountains retain Lakota names. The traditional Lakota game of buffalo and antelope graze together with cattle and sheep, and bison ranching is increasing on the Great Plains. Numerous monuments honour Lakota and European-American heroes and events.   Taken from https://en.wikipedia.org/wiki/Great_Sioux_Reservation

Modern Sioux

In 1980, the US Supreme Court ruled that the Sioux Indians were entitled to an award of $17.5 million, plus 5% interest per year since 1877, totalling about $106 million in compensation for the unjust taking of the Black Hills and in direct contravention of the Treaty of Fort Laramie. The Sioux have refused to take the money and it sits in a trust fund in Washington, collecting interest.

Today, there is division among the Sioux as to whether to claim the money, therefore relinquishing their rights to the Black Hills forever, or to press for the return of the Black Hills.

Details above taken from https://www.legendsofamerica.com/na-sioux/

SITTING BULL LIVES ON

Public Domain Image

Sitting Bull Lives On

 There is no doubt that Sitting Bull was, and still is, a legend.

He had a great deal of courage and although other Chiefs such as Crazy Horse were famous for their warrior skills, Sitting Bull possessed so much more. His powers to communicate with the spirits made him in the words of a tribe member 'big medicine'. A compliment indeed.

He was a great man. And he earned that greatness through his words and deeds as a Chief and a holy man. A man who believed and was true to the cardinal virtues and values of the Hunkpapa guiding his people that way.

But his courage was great too and came to the fore on many occasions. On one particular incident in 1872, it was reported that ***"during a battle with soldiers protecting railroad workers on the Yellowstone River, Sitting Bull led four other warriors out between the lines, sat calmly sharing a pipe with them as bullets buzzed around, carefully reamed the pipe out when they were finished, and then casually walked away."*** Courage, bravery, and strength in the face of danger.

He was also known for his generosity, a cardinal virtue also, which continued into his later life, and for his care and devotion to his family members. Add all these character traits together and you can then understand why he was a highly respected man held in very high esteem. All making him the ideal choice as the most respected Indian leader of the Plains, as he later was to become.

He also was an artist recording some of his victories in pictographs. We still use pictographs today in images for signs such as; disabled toilets signs, no smoking signs, café or no entry signs.

Public Domain Image

One of his famous pictographs is his counting coup at the age of fourteen. Sadly I do not have the copyright to show you the actual pictograph but above is a similar pictograph. But like all artists, Sitting Bull signed his pictographs. But not with his signature. With a buffalo drawing.

On the right you will see my interpretation of his pictograph signature as again I do not have the copyright to use the actual image. But you can see from the drawing, although much larger than the actual one, just exactly what he was drawing.

Here are a few quotes from the great man himself.

Let us put our minds together and see what life we can make for our children.

The white man knows how to make everything, but he does not know how to distribute it.

Behold, my friends, the spring is come; the earth has gladly received the embraces of the sun, and we shall soon see the results of their love!

When I was a boy, the Sioux owned the world. The sun rose and set on their land; they sent ten thousand men to battle. Where are the warriors today? Who slew them? Where are our lands? Who owns them?

God made me an Indian.

I wish it to be remembered that I was the last man of my tribe to surrender my rifle.

If we must die, we die defending our rights.

If the Great Spirit had desired me to be a white man, he would have made me so in the first place.

I have lived a long time, and I have seen a great deal, and I have always had a reason for everything I have done. Every act of my life has had an object in view, and no man can say that I have neglected facts or failed to think.

Sitting Bull

Public Domain Image

A Quote from Annie Oakley

The contents of his pockets were often emptied into the hands of small, ragged little boys, nor could he understand how so much wealth should go brushing by, unmindful of the poor.

Sitting Bull may have died a very long time ago, but his name will always live on and the man will be remembered forever.

"As individual fingers we can easily be broken, but all together we make a mighty fist." And they did make a mighty fist. Even now the Great Sioux Nation are strong together.

© Mick Stothard 2020

Public Domain Image

BIBLIOGRAPHY

Books Used as Reference

- Living in Two Worlds by Charles Eastman
- Bury My Heart at Wounded Knee by Dee Brown
- A Boy Called Slow by Joseph Bruchac
- The Lance and the Shield – The Life and Times of Sitting Bull – Robert M Utley
- Wooden Leg - A Warrior Who Fought Custer T. B. Marquis
- Sitting Bull: His Life and Legacy Ernie LaPointe
- The Life and Adventures of Frank Grouard, Chief of Scouts USA

Research Websites

- https://en.wikipedia.org/wiki/James_Morrow_Walsh
- https://www.pbs.org
- https://www.archives.gov/education/lessons/sioux-treaty
- https://en.wikipedia.org/wiki/Great_Sioux_Reservation
- http://siouxme.com/nativeamerican.html
- https://en.wikipedia.org/wiki/Sitting_Bull
- https://www.ducksters.com/history/native_americans/sitting_bull.php
- https://griid.org/2011/09/08/this-day-in-resistance-history-sitting-bull%E2%80%99s-railway-speech/
- https://www.history.com/topics/native-american-history/sitting-bull
- https://www.britannica.com/biography/Sitting-Bull
- https://www.pbs.org/weta/thewest/people/s_z/sittingbull.htm
- https://www.britannica.com/topic/American-frontier : How the West was won
- www.historynet.com/sitting-bull
- https://www.lyricfind.com/ - The Black Hills Of Dakota – Doris Day
- https://en.wikipedia.org/wiki/Wild_West_shows
- https://en.wikipedia.org/wiki/Annie_Oakley
- https://en.wikipedia.org/wiki/James_McLaughlin_(Indian_agent)
- https://en.wikipedia.org/wiki/Caroline_Weldon
- https://en.wikipedia.org/wiki/Wounded_Knee_MassacreWounded Knee Massacre
- https://www.legendsofamerica.com/na-sittingbull/
- https://www.legendsofamerica.com/na-sioux/

- https://www.brainyquote.com/quotes/sitting_bull_260481
- https://en.wikipedia.org/wiki/1868_in_the_United_Kingdom
- https://en.wikipedia.org/wiki/1890_in_the_United_Kingdom
- https://amertribes.proboards.com/thread/167/sitting-bull?page=5
- https://en.wikipedia.org/wiki/Mary_Collins_(missionary)
- https://www.encyclopedia.com/places/britain-ireland-france-and-low-countries/british-and-irish-political-geography/sitting-bull
- https://en.wikipedia.org/wiki/Jean-Louis_L%C3%A9gar%C3%A9
- https://en.wikipedia.org/wiki/Battle_of_Killdeer_Mountain
- https://en.wikipedia.org/wiki/Battle_of_the_Rosebud
- https://study.com/academy/lesson/sitting-bull-facts-history-timeline.html
- https://sittingbull.edu/about-sitting-bull/
- https://www.history.com/topics/native-american-history/sitting-bull
- https://www.azquotes.com/quote/1172232 Quote from Annie Oakley
- https://en.wikipedia.org/wiki/Sitting_Bull#/media/File:Sitting_Bull_Signature.svg
- https://en.wikipedia.org/wiki/1868_in_the_United_Kingdom   -cite_note-Pocket_On_This_Day-1

Images Used

Page 2 Cradleboard

Birmingham Museum of Art
(https://commons.wikimedia.org/wiki/File:Cradleboard
_of_the_Kiowa_or_Comanche_people.jpg)
Cradleboard of the Kiowa or Comanche people.
https://creativecommons.org/licenses/by/3.0/legalcode

Page 4 Buffalo Anatomy.
Gordon Johnson from Pixabay

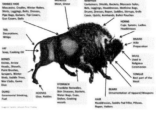

Page 8 Louisiana Purchase

William Morris (https://commons.wikimedia.org/wiki/File:Louisiana_Purchase.jpg)
https://creativecommons.org/licenses/by-sa/4.0/legalcode

Page 12 Her Holy Door (his
Mother) and one of his
daughters Many Horses

Von Bern https://commons.wikimedia.org/wiki/
File:Sitting_Bull_and_Family_while_at_Fort_Randall_summer_or_fall_1881.jpg
https://creativecommons.org/licenses/by-sa/4.0/legalcode

Page 33 Gold

https://www.victorianplaces.com.au/north-warrandyte
https://commons.wikimedia.org/wiki/File:Gold-miners-in-the-river.jpg
https://creativecommons.org/licenses/by-sa/4.0/legalcode

Page 74 Fort Burford

FlintWestwood
https://commons.wikimedia.org/wiki/File:Fort_Buford_Barracks_2010.jpg
Fort Buford Barracks 2010, https://creativecommons.org/licenses/by-sa/3.0/legalcode

Page 87 Buffalo - Ria Sopala from Pixabay

Page 114 Sitting Bull

Guerinf
https://commons.wikimedia.org/wiki/File:Sitting_Bull,_Notman.jpg
https://creativecommons.org/licenses/by-sa/4.0/legalcode

Page 80, 134 Sitting Bull

© Mick Stothard 2020

Throughout

Image by Clker-Free-Vector-Images from Pixabay

ALSO AVAILABLE BY CAROL DEAN

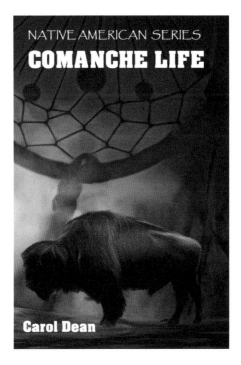

The Comanche were the fiercest and most feared of tribes. A warring tribe.

And a tribe, a people, fighting to preserve their traditions, values and the land they loved.

Find out how such a tribe lived their everyday lives, and how the Comanche almost fell into obscurity with the help of the 'white man', and how they rose again to be the Comanche Nation that they are today.

Available in hardback or paperback – black and white or colour

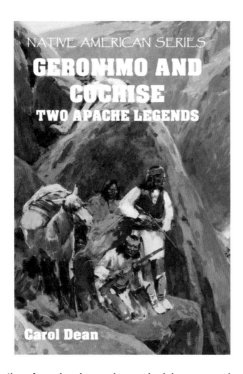

Over the years the Apache have been led by many legendary people. Two well known Apache legends, and the two that I have chosen to write about, are Geronimo and Cochise.

They lived in turbulent times. Times when these two legends needed to join forces to fight for their lands and the lives of their people against the Mexican and the American soldiers. Both forces seeking revenge and retribution for the deaths of loved ones at the hands of the white man's army, and the loss of their sacred lands desecrated by the white man.

Geronimo and Cochise's joint forces became a daring, dynamic and powerful fighting force to be reckoned with and feared.

This is their story.

Available in hardback or paperback – black and white or colour

.

Printed in Poland
by Amazon Fulfillment
Poland Sp. z o.o., Wrocław

64311412R00088